the unknown face

a memoir of marriage, mental illness, and the search for why

Gregory Duncan

the unknown face:
A memoir of marriage, mental illness, and the search for why

Copyright © 2023 by Gregory Duncan

ISBN (paperback) 979-8-9888602-0-4
ISBN (hardcover) 979-8-9888602-2-8
ISBN (ebook) 979-8-9888602-1-1
ISBN (audiobook) 979-8-9888602-3-5

Edited by William Kenower / Anne Dubuisson
Proofreading by Sarrah Kam [Paper Polish]
Cover and interior design by DTPerfect Book Design
Front cover image: *The Kiss* by Gustav Klimt

Published by New Origins Publishers

Contact the author at gregoryduncanauthor.com

Contents

Author's Note

WHILE THE CONVERSATIONS in this story might not be exactly the same words that were spoken, they are as close as I can remember and true to the meaning and intent at that time. All events are true, and occurrences where I was not present were relayed to me by family members.

The names of individuals have been changed when appropriate.

G.D.

*This is the only real concern of
the artist, to recreate out of the disorder
of life that order which is art.*

—JAMES BALDWIN / Autobiographical Notes
from *Notes of a Native Son*

Chapter 1
Spring Before Summer

Feel flooded by my emotions this week. Don't have direction and not happy without the prospect of being happy.

Not a lot of control in my life.

The things I want in life I ruined and I'm having a hard time making sense of life.

I don't feel like I've done the things I want, but things I feel obligated to do.

I'm not excited about anything or anything in the future.

Having a baby seems like a hassle.

Buying a house seems like a hassle.

I don't feel like I can do anything else because my identity is so wrapped up in what I do.

Don't feel like there is a lot of meaning in my life.

ON APRIL 3RD, 2018, my thirty-three-year-old wife, Rachel, wrote down some notes in her MacBook Pro. She frequently recorded her thoughts, as well as notes about the private trumpet lessons she taught. While I was not aware of what she wrote until sometime later, the message from that day in April was similar to things she had told me before in one way or another. We learned to manage and navigate her feelings, though the torrent that ran beneath was strong. Over time, the sympathy that I initially felt, and the overwhelming need to protect her, became intertwined with the monotony of everyday life.

We lived in a modern apartment complex, located on a hill in a small college town in Virginia. Except for the entrance, it was surrounded by thick woods, and nature had a way of impinging on the overly white, vibrant apartment community. We had moved there during our second year of marriage, and it seemed to be a great place to settle in before transitioning to a house of our own.

One of my daily chores was to take the dogs outside for their morning walk. This took place before work, around 6:30 a.m. or so. That spring, before all the rain started that summer, the two dogs and I set out on the path that eventually led to a big grassy stretch of land, which dropped off on one side to form a steep hill. Most mornings the grass would be filled with cold dew, and we would return with wet feet and paws. To the right of the path was our building, where each front door had two white pillars on either side—on the surface, it was an ideal place to live for young professionals who had time to invest in themselves; underneath, it was similar to any other apartment complex where things break and maintenance issues need to be addressed. When we got to the side of the building, my anxiety level increased—I needed to brace myself because there was a tree around the corner and there would often be a squirrel in the general vicinity. Cookie, a two-year-old black-and-white pointer, would pull, bark, and go crazy whenever she saw the squirrel, and day after day of having this same surprise around the corner became annoying. Our older black-and-brindle mutt, Hershey, was so mild mannered that it wouldn't affect him as much, though he also liked chasing squirrels.

One day, another surprise had been waiting for us after we made that turn. In the corner apartment that had a bedroom in the back with a sliding glass door facing the backyard, there was an older man who was catatonic and laying in a specialized bed. He was maybe in his late 50's or 60's, and almost always there in plain sight—placed by the attendant nurse, who provided him with a nice view of the thick forest and steep hill. When I glanced at him I discerned a blank, vacant face with short, straight hair. If he was any other person, my reaction would have been to say hello and I suppose that's what my reaction should've been—being nice for congeniality's sake. However, he couldn't say hello back and it threw off my typical exchange. I soon learned to ignore him and avoid the awkwardness every time we turned that corner.

It hadn't been easy to ignore him either. He was right there facing us, looking out through that sliding glass door every time we turned the corner. His face would stare straight ahead like a statue while his body lay at an angle in the slightly propped-up bed. I didn't actually know if he was asleep or looking, but his eyes were always in the back of my mind. They were the only thing in him that seemed to have life—the only thing that functioned like it should. My reaction to the man was similar to how people often see each other regardless of circumstances or familiarity. You see them and then you don't. You take in their presence, their being, and then you look away. Usually you can only see part of somebody; and almost always, you never truly see somebody for who they really are.

One day late that May, when the two dogs and I turned that corner on our morning walk, we were not greeted by an uncomfortable-yet-familiar presence, or by the sight of someone in the peripheral vision sitting, sleeping, watching TV, or looking out at the backyard. This time the room was empty. The blinds were still open, yet the character behind the curtain had disappeared. The next day and the day after that the room would still be empty, and I thought back to our initial encounters and how I had wanted to say hello but instead chose to ignore him. For a couple months we had each had a view of the other, separated by a thin pane of glass, and each time was like an introduction to a reality beyond comprehension. I wished I'd had the courage to look at him and acknowledge his presence. I wished I had waved hello, but I was too scared and ashamed to see something right in front of me that I couldn't accept.

The previous evening Rachel had come to me with her dilemma. Standing across from her in our small dining room, with the kitchen bar stools to my right and the large round dining room table to my left, I first greeted the dogs—my normal routine when coming home from work. After the typical chitchat, our conversation led to something that had probably been on her mind most of the day.

"Do you think our marriage therapy is going to fix our problems?" she asked me. She didn't feel a connection with me and was struggling to feel like we were in a productive relationship. The signs of dysfunction she pointed to had been slowly developing, and it did seem like we had lost that spark in our marriage. For me, it was difficult to be a second-year teacher, make the forty-minute commute to work every day, and still be a musician as well as a husband. The reality was that ever since I started teaching high school Spanish two years prior, I had lost a part of myself because I was so busy working. It had become harder to be the same person I used to be, in a new location, with a new job and little time for music or family. For the first ten years of my professional career, I had worked as a musician, and gradually taught more to earn a stable income. As my teaching responsibilities grew, it became harder to make time for music—I knew I was living the life I chose, though I also wondered if somehow life chose me.

Rachel had fiery, long, red hair, and inquisitive thick lips. When she asked me the question, her lips were slightly open—which usually meant she was worried or uncertain—not pursed tightly like when she was angry or contemplative. I stood in front of her, unexpectedly transfixed. I probably should have been more worried about her question, but instead I was focused on her lips and smiled slightly. I knew from experience to choose my words carefully and not mention her lips—she usually got annoyed when I commented on their shape, calling my response trivial or evasive.

"Yeah," I replied. "But I still think we should try to do more fun things together. Do you remember when I mentioned getting a Wii?"

She rolled her eyes at me. "That's not going to help. Are you still serious about that?" she asked.

"The routine is too much: get up, go to work, come home, make small talk, eat dinner, prepare for the next day, go to bed," I said. "It used to be a good way to have fun when we played with friends in Chicago, why not now?"

Wii was a gaming system that was no longer as popular. It had a motion sensor that read a hand-held remote, so you were inevitably moving around and being crazy in a good way. One day back in March we had gone to the nearest GameStop store, but they didn't have anything at a good price. We walked silently back to our car and while getting inside, I said:

"Do you want to go to another place to find a Wii system?"

I hoped she would agree, but had a sinking feeling she wouldn't.

"A Wii isn't going to solve our problems. I can't see myself getting into it," she replied with a hint of hopelessness. "I need to connect with you by talking about things that are meaningful. We just sit at the dinner table and talk about boring stuff."

As we pulled out of the lifeless parking lot I resigned to working more on our conversations. But it was as if I was being forced to do something I wasn't trained to do. My mind took jabs at me: "Be more like a girl"; "Express your feelings." As we drove, the best way home eluded me once again. "Do I go back on Barracks or take Emmet Street?" I asked her.

"Take Emmet," she said, still baffled at my inability to become familiar with our new town, as well as my inability to use Google Maps.

"OK, we can talk more about deep things then," I said. But how? My voice sounded perturbed and stubbornly defiant. Having strong opinions on politics, health care, or societal issues wasn't exactly my forte. My wife really just wanted less of the surfacy, casual conversations I was used to, and more of something that came from feeling something. Unfortunately, feeling something wasn't exactly my forte either.

Earlier that month, a week or so before our trip to GameStop, Rachel had been busy planning a music festival at the university, where she was an accomplished professor of trumpet. Her pedigree included attending one of the most prestigious music conservatories in the country, performing with numerous orchestras worldwide, and knowing almost everyone in the business (or so it seemed to me). She had an "it" factor in terms of her effect on a musical ensemble due to her in-depth knowledge of style—leading orchestras with a sound and spirit that demonstrated how the music was supposed to be played.

For the festival, she helped coordinate the workshops and all the logistics, including travel and accommodations for the performers. She also organized the concert, which served as the culmination of the festival, wherein a thirty-or-so piece brass ensemble performed on stage for a small, but awe-inspired, crowd. It featured the invited performers plus the student musicians who participated in the workshops. Trumpets, trombones, tubas, and French horns all worked in unison to grab the audience's attention and let them know how classical music can be so subtle and yet in your face at the same time. Prior to the performance of the enormous brass ensemble, the invited performers, known as the New Chicago Brass, played in a somewhat smaller group (if you consider ten musicians a small group). From the moment they played the first song they steamrolled through their repertoire like consummate professionals. They played one amazing song after another and I didn't think I could be more impressed, until the final moment of the concert.

At that point, Rachel directed the group of almost thirty brass musicians in a rendition of a baroque piece by the Italian composer Gabrieli. She stood at the front of the stage and faced the large, eager group assembled in a U-shape formation. She smiled at the musicians with a knowing gleam in her eyes. The ensemble shape matched the U-shaped wall behind the stage, which showcased a large fresco of Raphael's classic Renaissance painting, "The School of Athens." With the colorful depiction of ancient philosophers as a backdrop, Rachel raised her arms to conduct. Plato was in the fresco above to her left, and Aristotle was to her right. I sat in awe of my wife as I took a video of the performance. She skillfully took what she learned in her conducting class from graduate school and led the band with confidence, grace, and poise. It was the highlight of the concert, which was no small feat considering all of the exceptional prior performances. I shared the video with her via Facebook after the concert in an attempt to show my admiration.

When she came backstage, I approached her with a polite half smile and, after waiting for her to finish talking with one or two others, I said:

"Nice job. I just posted a video of you on Facebook." She paused a little, her mouth repeating my own half smile. "Thanks," she said before moving on to another person. She was used to my stiff and unemotional congratulations after her performances and probably couldn't read the small amount of emotion that emanated from my face and voice. On that day I tried to show that I saw her for her talent and was proud. Instead, she questioned my intent and ignored my compliment. The emotional language necessary to reach her usually evaded me. Once again, I felt lost and defeated, as if I was fighting a battle I was destined to lose. "Isn't this what she wants?" I asked myself. "Why isn't she more pleased?"

Despite my lack of emotional connection with my wife, I did try. It was perhaps a stilted effort, but it was all that I could muster. One such conversation would be like the one we had one warm evening later on in May.

"I feel weird every time I go to these high school commencements," I said as we sat down for dinner around our circular glass table. We had deliberated about what to eat that evening and had finally settled on a typical meal of grilled chicken, broccoli, and rice.

"What do you mean?" she asked.

"I don't know. There's no place for the teachers to sit and I just stand there like I don't belong and listen to people give speeches who don't know how to give speeches."

Rachel gave me a blank stare. "Well they're in high school."

"Not all," I replied. "The adults give speeches too. Everyone just reads from their page and there's no feeling in it or looseness to it. It's like they're playing a part without knowing why."

"Maybe you're too hard on them," she said. There was a slight pause as she turned over a piece of broccoli. She continued: "What do you think about buying a house next year?"

"Oh, I don't have any strong opinions," I said looking downward. "Why?"

"Don't you think we should be looking as soon as possible?" she replied with a hint of disappointment.

"Yeah, I guess so. I'm just busy with school," I said.

Rachel got quiet and for the rest of the dinner we talked very little. In typical fashion, I said what little I could and had little to add to what she was interested in. Later on, I did try to engage her in more serious topics—ones that weren't mundane or too much like small talk.

"Hey, what do you think about the healthcare crisis?" I asked one evening. "It's all a mess. I mean, the health insurance companies might as well be holding up people at gunpoint saying, 'Your money or your life.'"

"Umm, yes I agree," she replied, indicating her mind was somewhere else. "It sucks," she added. "It would've been nice if you could've been more sympathetic the time I cut my finger and had a gigantic hospital bill."

My reply took awhile. "Well, sorry about that. I'm not good with sympathy. What do you think should be done about health care?"

Rachel looked puzzled—not puzzled because she didn't know how to reply. She was bewildered because she knew intuitively that I didn't want to be talking about health care—my forced effort at conversation lacked the feeling and spontaneity that she craved. It was a moment when our family backgrounds, or the way we were used to communicating and connecting, suddenly collided and then couldn't find common ground.

My family played pinochle and board games; her family sat around and talked to each other in a pleasant, Midwestern way that made one feel both at peace and on edge at the same time. I had adapted to adulthood by turning into a turtle and learning how to disappear; she'd adapted to adulthood by turning into a dog and learning how to charm. I was the reticent, introverted artist; she was the gregarious, determined professional.

"They need to fix it fast—and I think you're trying too hard," she said. "We're still not connecting because I don't feel anything from you."

One rainy day later that spring, we showed up at our marriage therapist's office for our third session. There were multiple degrees showcased on the wall, and along with the couch: an armchair and an expensive wood desk with a businesslike chair. To the left of the couch where both Rachel and I sat was a bookcase full of psychology books, and along one of the shelves, in front of the books, were small figurines of the characters from the Wizard of Oz. I meant to ask the therapist about them but always forgot amidst the turmoil we discussed in our sessions.

The therapist, sitting in the armchair across from us, was a short, older man who looked like he could have also been an accountant or perhaps a salesman. He reminded me for some reason of Willy Loman in *Death of a Salesman*. He liked to quote famous psychologists and, after hearing both sides of our stories, he stated:

"The famous psychologist Elvin Semrad once said, 'The greatest sources of our suffering are the lies we tell ourselves.' Most human suffering is related to love and loss, and my job is to help both of you acknowledge, experience, and bear the reality of life—with all its pleasures and heartbreak. I appreciate both of your stories and am glad that both of you could open up to me."

"You know..." he hesitated a little before continuing.

"There was another famous psychiatrist from France named Pierre Janet and he once said, 'Every life is a piece of art, put together with all means available.' Both of you are doing the best that you can and the more you realize and appreciate what your partner is going through, the more you will be able to find common ground and overcome difficulties."

He had Rachel dive deeper into what was troubling her about our relationship. At one point she broke down and sobbed a little, unable to continue. I put my hand on her leg for support and explained to the therapist what she was trying to say and how she felt. It was the same story Rachel had told me many times. She was probably surprised I understood since it contrasted with my normal aloof reaction. The difficulty for Rachel was identifying her feelings and communicating them. The therapist worked with her on that before turning his attention to me.

"Greg, after hearing your story, I don't think you like conflict. And, after listening to Rachel, I think this keeps you from reaching out to her more when she's pushing at you to get more out of you. What are some ways you can meet her halfway? Rachel should learn how to avoid pushing so hard, but that being said, you also need to learn to respond better to those pushes."

It was always easy to know what to do and say in the therapist's office. But when we got home and continued on with our lives, it was difficult to put into practice things we were learning in our sessions. Perhaps without another person present, it was easy for me to put back up my defenses and avoid the uncomfortable feelings within. Rachel continued to push and I continued to retreat. It was frustrating because it always seemed like two steps forward and one step backwards. What we didn't realize was that there were deeper issues preventing our relationship from taking the next step—issues I would read about a year or so later in more in-depth, detailed psychology books. Every time we got close to the true center of our identities or we became closer as a couple, something usually happened and one of us would self-destruct. There was something underneath it all, waiting to surface.

Chapter 2
Dating

...we only love—that which is like ourselves and in so far as it is like ourselves, and the more like it is the more we love...
—Miguel de Unamuno, Poet

ACHEL WAS THE kind of person everyone wanted to be around, mainly because she was good at relating to people. That was how she got her energy, from other people. She said her spirit animal was a golden retriever and that was true. There were many times when she would plop on my lap seeking attention, much like the smiley, happy-go-lucky dog. She would be content and at peace, as if sitting on someone's lap relieved her from the consternation of being by herself. Her eyes would shine and her face would become serene, like she had transformed into a doll—it seemed that no thoughts entered into her head in those moments. A common story her mother liked to tell is of constantly carrying around baby Rachel, who was pleased to be so close to her mom. The moment she was left by herself or separated, she would become upset.

As an adult, Rachel enjoyed finding out what made people tick and then having deep conversations with them about life. When she came back from a music festival that summer, where she had worked as a coach and mentor, she told me about a game she set up in her hotel room. Everyone hung out in her room and if someone sat on the "share bed," they had to share something personal or vulnerable about themselves. That was Rachel—always trying to get to the heart of the matter and form connections as quickly as possible. Sometimes it would be uncomfortable for me, but it's what she enjoyed doing almost more than anything. I used to joke with her that I should buy her a t-shirt that said, "I'm an overshare bear."

On one occasion while first dating, we were backstage after one of my gigs in Milwaukee at its annual Summerfest. We were milling around, casually talking to band members as they passed by. The atmosphere was warm and crowded and the backstage area was like a blue, metallic maze. I was thinking about how to get to my car and how to get paid—the two most important things musicians think about after a gig. Probably because she was bored, Rachel looked for anyone to engage in a conversation with her, and we found a congenial, tall bass player who obliged. He played in a different group, but nonetheless was there with a friend, just passing by.

There was a minute of pleasantries and regular social dialogue and then the conversation somehow turned into religion and religious fanatics. Rachel pounced.

"Jesus was a man!" she said with a charged voice and radiant face. She pointed out that she had a Jewish background and wasn't raised to consider Jesus as the be-all and end-all.

The bass player laughed and agreed. He didn't understand religious zealots either. Rachel began to explain her history with fanatics and as she continued, I cringed—not because what she was saying wasn't interesting, valid, or even socially acceptable. I recoiled because I didn't know the bass player that well (she didn't either, having just met him), and it wasn't the typical conversation you have when you're just passing by exchanging small talk. But Rachel dove in headfirst. She usually would. The bass player didn't seem to mind, likely not sharing my discomfort.

"Hey Rachel, we have to go get my car before there's too much traffic," I said, looking for an excuse to leave. After probably another minute or so of chatting, I was able to convince her to leave. When she found someone to connect with, and when she was engaged in a real conversation (not your routine fake, surfacy chats), she wanted that moment to last forever. I, on the other hand, hoped those moments wouldn't last too long.

My longest relationship before meeting Rachel had lasted less than a year. I was a musician, private trumpet instructor, and taught ESL classes as a part-time job. I didn't make a lot of money, was not super assertive, and didn't have a plethora of self-confidence. More importantly however, I didn't know how to follow my heart, and didn't know how to continue believing in myself when faced with rejection and the different obstacles that life likes to set up like little landmines, waiting to catch you when you don't expect it.

When I met Rachel in 2010, I had recently come back from a year abroad in Spain. After five years in Chicago (I had moved there around 2004), I was fed up and ready for a change of scenery. My almost year-long relationship had ended, I wasn't making any progress with my music career, and I didn't seem to have the kinds of friends or close relationships I needed. If life's journey took place in a moving vehicle, I was always looking for the ejection seat—escaping when things got bumpy or out of control.

We met while playing intramural softball in a league located on the north side of town. We both played baseball when we were younger and since we had some mutual friends, we ended up on the same team one day. When I saw her the first time, she was immediately on my radar. Who was this pretty redhead playing on an intramural softball team? That probably was not the case for her, however. In a story relayed to me later on, Rachel had a friend who occasionally played on the team and on that day, this friend picked Rachel up to go to the game and came by to pick me up as well. Before swinging by my apartment, both girls had an opportunity to chat.

"Are there any cute guys on the team?" Rachel had asked.

"No, not really," her friend had replied.

It was a warm, sunny day in September and the cooler fall weather hadn't quite arrived yet. I got in the car wearing sweatpants and a wrinkled, faded t-shirt. While I clean up nicely, I imagine I probably didn't look my best when going to play softball that Saturday morning.

As far as the game, we lost but put up a good fight. Rachel made some good plays, including digging out some tough grounders at second base and throwing the runner out. After the game we went to a local bar in the Lakeview neighborhood to socialize and have a beer. I sat to the right of her place at the head of the table and found out more about her. Everybody on the team wanted her to come back and play since she was only subbing—she also was in demand because she was fun to hang out with. She didn't seem to get caught up in any form of social anxiety or awkwardness like the rest of us, and she knew just when to lighten the mood with humor.

One reason I still wasn't on Rachel's radar was because I always tried to be subtle. I guess that to say that I'm a subtle person would be an understatement—while dating at that time, I was more like a spy who tried to never tip their hand. It caused confusion because usually when I was hitting on a girl, she thought I was making small talk. If I was making small talk, she thought I was hitting on her. Somewhere along the line of not tipping my hand I got my signals crossed. I think on that day, Rachel thought I was making small talk. Here was some scruffy guy who didn't talk much about himself, asking her questions. I let on that I played the trumpet as well and suggested I help her some time with a jazz solo she was trying to learn. We agreed to potentially set that up and I tried to continue communication via Facebook.

Rachel went to play a couple gigs with the Philadelphia Orchestra in October, so I continued to be off her radar. It was easy to try to become friends with a fellow trumpet player such as Rachel because trumpet players always stick together, like being a part of a fraternity of sorts. The fact that she was a girl playing with the

Philadelphia Orchestra increased her uniqueness and value. How could I not get to know her better?

By November, we had decided to scrap the idea of a jazz lesson and went out to hear some live music instead. She didn't even know it was a date. But when I stepped out of my apartment all cleaned up and holding the same trumpet case she owned, things changed. I told her I might sit in with the band at a Lakeview bar called "Alive One," and I think she was impressed. A connection started to take shape.

She picked me up that clear November night by driving to the cul-de-sac on Malden Street, where I lived in a large, U-shaped brick apartment building. The smell of fall was all around, with dying leaves and small patches of grass ready to hibernate for the winter. The grass and trees around the building were guarded by a black gate, keeping visitors and tenants at a distance as if it were a well-preserved nature park. I wore a scarf and a black jacket picked out for me by an ex-girlfriend and as I walked out the entrance, passed the fence, and jumped in her car carrying a trumpet case made by the Rocky Mountain Case Company, Rachel said to me:

"Hey, that's the same trumpet case I have!"

"Oh, really? Yeah, you don't see too many of these," I replied. The medium-sized black case had a lot of space and good insulation, just not a good zipper. At some point the company had stopped making them.

"That's crazy that you have the same one," she said. "Yeah I love that case. I don't know why more people don't have one. What do you like best about it?" We continued talking about trumpet stuff for a few moments longer, and then connected further by talking about musical tastes.

When we got to the bar, the atmosphere was dark and intense. The only window in the back music room was covered with a black curtain, and large, phantom-like black-and-white paintings covered the walls. The fusion band played a frenetic style—the modern groove coming from the electric bass and piano zipped around each corner of the room while the saxophone dazzled the crowd with flurries of notes. It really wasn't my bag (or, "not my specialty" in regular speak) and I would be lying if I said I wasn't intimidated by the contemporary groove and virtuosic displays of musical prowess. As a result, I didn't end up playing with the band that night. After about an hour of listening and chatting with my friend, who played saxophone, Rachel and I left and had a great time going to different bars and hearing other live music.

When we went back to my apartment I demonstrated to her how inadequate I was at putting on my scarf—I couldn't tie a scarf, or otherwise figure out how to properly wear one. She thought it was so funny that we probably messed around with that scarf for half an hour. Part of Rachel's sense of humor was finding amusement in people's quirks, and she definitely latched onto my scarf antics as comedic relief. We both laughed a lot that night and got along great. I could be myself around her and she seemed to understand my sense of humor, so we continued to see each other off and on for the next couple of months.

Sometime later that fall we met at Nick's on Wilson. It was a dive bar just down the street from my studio apartment on Malden, and the kind of place that seemed like it should have been more popular than it was. The wood sign outside featured a giant pineapple in between "Nick's" and "on Wilson", which demonstrated the oddity of the place since it gave the appearance of a dive bar trying to be something else.

The interior was long and narrow like one wide corridor. Just to the left of the black and brown bar was a lit-up wall devoted to a giant painting, a mural of sorts. The colorful scene made the bar seem hip, even though the picture appeared out of place. Two young characters danced in the middle of a city street. Two attractive females were on either side of a boy, who danced with his arms up in the air, body contorted to the groove he felt. The woman on the left danced to her own inner groove—her arms were outstretched with hands mimicking the rhythm, her butt pushed out with knees slightly bent. The lady on the right pushed down the lever to a large barrel of gin and looked seductively to the side like she knew something the others didn't. The liquid poured out of the barrel and surrounded the dancers as if the alcohol was providing the beat. The two characters danced uninhibited amidst a spell of flowing gin, but neither one was really dancing with the other—only dancing their own separate dances.

"Hey, how was your day?" Rachel asked as we sat at the bar.

"All right, nothing special," I replied, looking at her seated to my right and then down at my drink. "Went to the library and checked out some books the other day, so I just started to read some of them."

"Oh, really? What books?" she asked, looking at me intently.

"Some psychology books about this famous psychologist named Carl Jung," I replied.

"Cool," she said. "Why those books?"

"He was really into dreams and the subconscious and since I just started writing down my own dreams, the books help me interpret them a little," I said, feeling proud of the knowledge I had just gained.

"Is he like Freud? Didn't he think, like, everything had to do with sex?"

"No." I laughed. "Not quite like that. He separated himself from Freud at some point. He was more into dreams and symbols and what things mean on a deeper level."

"Very cool. I would like to understand my own dreams—they're so vivid and it's always like real life. I mean, I usually know when I'm dreaming," she said.

"Well, I bet the book I'm reading says something about that."

"What else did you read?"

"Just things like, if you dream about a house—the house probably represents part of your psyche or part of your inner self. Going to the bathroom part of the house would represent trying to "let go" of something in your life. Also, I read this cool story about how Jung had a patient who was a mountain climber. The mountain climber was telling Jung about a dream he had where he was climbing a large mountain and somehow made a misstep, resulting in a bad fall. After hearing the dream, Jung advised the man not to go on his next expedition, for fear that the subconscious was communicating something. Instead, the man went, and ended up dying in a similar climbing accident," I said.

"Whoa," she said. "Freaky."

"Yeah, it's crazy," I replied.

"I'm also into psychology. How'd you get into this stuff though?" she asked.

"Oh, just from when I was in college," I said. "I had problems with depression and took antidepressants. Since they didn't do anything except numb me out, and since the person I talked to didn't help any, I looked for other ways to figure things out."

"Yeah, I had to take antidepressants when I was in school too," she said.

"Really? What for?"

"Cause some people suck and school was hard," she said after thinking for a moment. "I stopped taking them several years ago." We continued chatting for a little while longer, closed the bill and walked back to my place, about ten minutes away.

"Rachel, it's late. I gotta go to sleep," I said with an exasperated tone about an hour later. We lay next to each other on top of the full-size bed that took up half the room in the small studio. The radiator at the other end of the room turned on with a slow, clanking noise—the kind of sound that was annoying at first but later turned into an odd sense of comfort through the constant repetition.

"I know, but I'm upset. Let's just talk a little bit more," she replied.

"OK, but ya know I have to be up by 6:30."

"I just need to talk about things. But like, you're not hearing me."

"Well, what do you want to talk about?"

She paused for a moment. "I just don't know why you can't be affectionate with me. Every time I touch your back, you freak out."

"Rachel, do we have to get into this right now?"

"Yeah, I don't understand you. I want to understand you, but you don't make sense."

"Listen, I have a sensitive lower back. I don't know why."

"Well, but like, I need to feel connected to you in a physical way and when you pull away it hurts. I feel rejected."

"I'm not rejecting you," I replied with a sigh of frustration. Eventually we would both fall asleep and I would crawl out of bed the next morning and off to work.

In the beginning of our relationship, we bonded over talking about dreams and social-emotional issues. I could help her a little and talk about things she dreamed about. One thing that was clear from our early conversations was that we were ready to leave past issues behind and be more mature in dealing with problems. Somehow, we thought we were past all of that. Over time, I stopped reading books about Jung and the subconscious. Life demanded more from me and I didn't have time. When Rachel kept asking me about her dreams and what things meant, it became harder to answer or give her insight. I wanted to be able to, but it was above my expertise. After awhile, I gave her the book by Jungian scholar James Hall and had her read the passage that might relate to her particular dream. After a while, her questions annoyed me. Soon, she stopped asking. I wanted to help her, but didn't know how.

One morning she woke up with tears in her eyes. Her distraught face was out of place for just waking up, and caught me off guard. She immediately needed consoling, though telling her it was just a dream didn't help that much. My reaction and tone of voice tried to be sympathetic but again, emotions weren't exactly my strong suit. Before getting out of bed that day, she slowly described the following dream and I didn't know what to make of it. Since I told her about writing my own dreams down, Rachel later did the same.

Stacy and Jim were convincing me I was a terrible friend and musician—they made me look so bad to others that they all believed them. I tried to plead my case and nobody believed me. I felt ganged up on even though I had never heard anything bad about my professionalism ever before. I felt like I was going crazy! I didn't realize "everybody" thought I was a terrible person. I was crying so hard and nobody cared. Thought about killing myself and right before I woke up, Stacy looked at me with a glimmer of remorse. This was not the Jim I knew to lash out. Greg had a hard time backing me up.

Chapter 3
The Unknown Face

Projections change the world into the replica of one's unknown face…It is an unconscious factor which spins the illusions that veil his world. And what is being spun is a cocoon, which in the end will completely envelop him.

—Carl Jung, Psychologist

WHEN SEARCHING FOR answers about one's life, it's usually helpful to go back to the beginning—to childhood, for example, the launch of a new chapter in one's life, or perhaps the origin of a new relationship. Things happen, things begin, things start anew. People don't think twice about the details. It's only after something goes wrong that one usually takes the time to reflect and put the pieces together. Feelings get buried. Thoughts get buried. Memories get buried. Time has a way of covering things over in a thick layer of regret and absentmindedness.

On one of those first dates in the winter of 2010, I explained to Rachel my Tootsie Roll Pop analogy of life. It was a chilly December night and we had already gone out many times that fall and developed a liking for each other. The Tootsie Roll Pop theory was a belief that everyone goes through life with an outer shell. Some people have thick shells while others have very thin ones. The shell is there to protect people from the dangers of life, things that might harm them. More importantly, the shell is there to keep something within from going out into the world. What is within is often a mystery to even the person themselves. But over time, the shell can be worn down, the chocolate center exposed. If the person is ready for that exposure then it can be a marvelous thing, but if they are not ready, it can be dangerous—dangerous maybe because they're not ready to be carried by the stream of life, or dangerous maybe because they're not ready to offer that which is within.

We went out to eat that December evening at a trendy Mexican restaurant downtown called Zocalo. The restaurant's exterior was just a plain, nondescript red brick building. You would have thought there was a business office inside if it weren't for the word "Restaurant" printed in white on the red awning. Upon entering, Zocalo transformed into a glamorous combination of colors—the light brown of the hardwood floor and tables blended with the long, dark mahogany bar and the dusky red-and-orange colored walls. The soft, evenly placed lighting created an elegant atmosphere and helped illuminate the countless bottles of tequila that sat behind the bar in a dark brown shelf. As we sat down at a round table not far from the entrance, the server came over and was immediately familiar. It was the same petite, frizzy-haired girl who had given me her phone number when I asked for it there months before meeting Rachel. She never replied to my couple of texts and my ego was still sore. The server of course was mature enough to pretend like she didn't recognize me and I wouldn't have been surprised if she had really forgotten. But I brought it up in front of Rachel because I was trying to prove that I had value.

"Hey, do you remember me from before?" I asked the server. She responded with a blank look.

"Yeah, you never replied to my texts," I continued. Again, she tried to plead ignorance, as if she never received any text from me or never would have reason to. She was probably trying to help me save face even if I wasn't eager to do that for myself. I wanted the waitress to see that I was with a date, and I used Rachel to prove that I wasn't a nobody.

Rachel took everything in stride. But she confessed to me later that she had almost broken things off with me the next day. She interpreted my actions as hitting on the waitress in front of her. During our dinner that night, I explained my Tootsie Roll Pop theory. Rachel misunderstood it because I didn't explain it very well; it was still an underdeveloped concept in my head. I also used the theory to explain dating, wherein each person basically had to date so many people before finding the right one, and you would only find the right one after your outer shell was worn down. Since our date coincided with the time I also told Rachel we should take a break (I was going back to Spain for a month in January), she took it the wrong way and assumed I was pointing out that she wasn't the right person.

"How am I really like a Tootsie Roll Pop?" I wondered that night when we came back to her place and watched the movie "Inception" while snuggled somewhat uncomfortably on her couch. On the outside I could be mysterious or understated—I knew there was more to me than that. So what was it and why couldn't I get to the core?

The irony was that that night I did show Rachel a side of myself that I wasn't comfortable showing—the side that was an immature selfish jerk. She recognized it immediately but by the time she processed what she saw, I went back to covering that part of myself up. Rachel was good at breaking through people's shells but in the entire time I knew her, she only got through part of mine. For some reason, I wasn't ready to uncover the rest.

I left for Spain on the first of January in 2011, excited to go back and reconnect with friends, and eager to play a couple concerts. She drove me to the airport that cold, wintry day with tears in her eyes. She also had car trouble after dropping me off, which made her day even worse. I didn't understand at the time how hard it was for her to deal with abandonment. To make matters worse, there were problems with my internet connection towards the end of the trip and Skyping with her became difficult. When February finally came, we had fallen out of touch. Upon my return to Chicago, I was greeted by a mountain of snow and uncertainty about my future dating life. A friend picked me up from the airport and when I finished telling him about my month-long adventure, the topic shifted to Rachel and if we were going to continue dating. I told him I didn't know but was still interested if she was.

Around a week later Rachel and I made plans to meet up and go see a movie. We got her favorite pizza at Pequod's, went to the downtown AMC theater, and basically picked up where we left off. I drove back to her place and parked the car in front of her Rogers Park apartment on Maplewood Avenue with snow piled up near the sidewalks. She lived there with two roommates from Northwestern, and her house was frequently a meeting spot for parties with many young aspiring classical musicians. I turned off the engine, and before we got out she said to me:

"I need to tell you something important and I don't know how." She fought back tears as best she could. "When you were in Spain, I slept with another person and that person gave me something I didn't want. I feel like my life is over and I understand if you don't want to be with me anymore."

"What do you mean?" I asked, getting concerned.

"I got an STD and the last few weeks have been just awful. You can ask my roommates. I've been a mess. I don't know if I can live anymore after something like this." The tears started to fall. She took a napkin and blotted her mascara. The anguish on her face was palpable.

My heart sank and I immediately wanted to help her. I suppose I also felt some guilt because something tugged at my soul. I didn't cause the situation she was in but I was somehow inadvertently part of it. The thing about Rachel and the other reason I couldn't run away was because her vulnerability drew me in—she possessed strength and fragility all at the same time. She just wasn't like any other girl I ever met and I wanted to know more about her.

"How did it happen?" I asked.

"Just being stupid and having unprotected sex with someone I didn't really know."

"Well, wait—why did that happen?" The car was getting colder and I could see her breath as she spoke.

"I was upset when you stopped contacting me from Spain and went out with some friends and started drinking. It just happened."

"Look, it's not that big a deal. We can still see each other, just have to figure things out," I said.

"Really? You don't have to continue to see me. I'd understand," she said.

"I know. But let's not end things—we can go slow and see what happens."

That night at least I provided what she needed at the moment—comfort. I just held her and gave her all the sympathy I could. In some ways, it was the same comfort and sympathy I longed for myself. It was a feeling that would become harder and harder to summon the longer our relationship lasted. She needed more emotion and comfort than I could give—especially when life got busy and I went on autopilot.

When I left later that night, she felt better. We later agreed to play it safe and continued to date. Some months later however, I also got an infection and her guilt ravaged her—mainly because at that point we weren't sure where the relationship was heading. I told her it wasn't that big of a deal, that somehow it was a fate I was comfortable with. It definitely didn't bother me as much as it did her, though sharing an STD definitely complicated things. All of a sudden, breaking up became harder and new alliances would be harder to form. For her, having an STD was almost like the end of the world, and it traumatized her to the point of trying group therapy once or twice. For me, it was something I was surprised I didn't have already. In the end, it didn't seem to matter because we agreed to keep going and put differences or complications aside.

One evening later that winter, Rachel shared some photos from her past. I think I had initially shared some photos of my own past and then not long after, we were in her apartment in Rogers Park when she dug up a box with some not-too-distant memories. The box contained a portfolio of poems that she wrote in high school and college and also a bunch of photos. With anxious hesitation she handed me an untitled poem and asked me to read it and give an honest opinion. I sat down on the long white couch in the dark, shadowy living room and tried to make sense of what I now held in my hand. The poem's lines and stanzas were printed from a computer that she probably also used in college. The prose was impressive because of its emotional poignancy.

"It's good," I told her, giving her a glance after looking up from the page. "What is this part talking about?" I asked, pointing to a part in the second stanza. "Is it in general or a specific moment?" She explained in such a way where I had to read between the lines—that she wrote it after losing her virginity to someone who would soon leave her. I was moved by her vulnerability but also didn't know what else to say.

She next dug up photos from the same box—some college pictures, some taken at different music festivals, and some photos of her with her family. There was one photo of her sitting in a tour bus, heading off to a performance somewhere in Japan. She had turned around in her seat, and was looking down, not at the camera. Her face looked contemplative, like she was considering who to talk to next or how to respond to someone. I almost didn't think it was her in the photo. The camera captured a side of her I had never seen.

"Is that really you in the photo?" I asked.

"Yeah," she said matter-of-factly. "I might have been mad or thinking about something." Her face seemed blank and vacant. The eyes were dark, both around the edges and inside. Instead of her normal attractive features, her lips seemed thinner, the skin even whiter, and the face perhaps flatter and less oval. It wasn't a case of no makeup because I was familiar with both made-up and bare faces and often preferred the latter. She really didn't need makeup, and used it to look more adult and less like a kid.

"Oh, it doesn't look like you at all," I said. "How come I never saw this side of her?" I wondered. "Why did she look so unfamiliar?" In all the time I knew her I never saw that face because it was something only exposed in a quick capture of the camera or a surprise short moment of video. I came to understand that the unknown face, like the layer hidden in the Tootsie Roll Pop, is usually never seen, for it does not want to be seen. I assumed that the face in the photo that day represented another part of her I wasn't familiar with. In my case, I kept my inner self pretty well hidden and can only guess that my unknown face was a mystery to those around me, including myself.

But the fascinating thing about Rachel was that she could become her inner self. More than anyone I ever met, she could live in that realm of buried thoughts and anxieties. The difference between Rachel and other people I knew was that the more you got to know her, the more she took off her mask. While I avoided my own unknown face at all costs, she was consumed by it. In moments when the veil came down, she lived on the edge of that stark nakedness more than anyone I knew. I never really saw the face of hers from the photograph in real life, perhaps because I *couldn't* see it, not physically anyway. I would see it in her words and actions.

The first time Rachel threw caution to the wind was when I got a call from a hospital in downtown Chicago. She had gone to a graduation party off of Michigan Avenue with her cousin and the staff had kept everyone's glasses full. Unfortunately, Rachel was what's known as a lightweight. She could drink a little, not a lot, and her body would shut down if she had too much. The next morning when I went to get her at Northwestern Memorial Hospital, she was lying in a bed with an IV in her arm, trying to rehydrate and sober up.

"Rachel, what happened?" I asked her, completely dumbfounded as to how she ended up in one of the gurney beds in a hallway with nurses and random medical personnel passing by every so often.

"I don't want to talk about it. Can you just take me home?" Her face was tired and stoic, a vivid contrast from her usually animated self.

"Yeah, of course," I replied.

"I have to wait for someone to come by and take this out," she said. Eventually a sympathetic nurse came by to discharge her and explained the situation. Apparently she had tried to make it to the train to get home but passed out on the stairs that led up to the train tracks. A Good Samaritan found her and took her to the hospital. She was lucky nothing worse happened to her physically, and she probably felt worse emotionally. She thought I might leave her since at that time our relationship was fairly new. I took her home from the hospital that morning and didn't know what to say. It was similar to when she told me about the STD because it was like there was an invisible hand trying to push me away and probably the first warning sign that something wasn't right. I knew other people that got blackout drunk, but usually they didn't need medical attention.

Instead of running away, I tried to look past the red flags in the relationship and focused on the positive things. After all, was I perfect? Did I have a track record of lasting relationships?

Chapter 4
Albany Park

It is this fear of the unconscious psyche which not only impedes self-knowledge but is the gravest obstacle to a wider understanding and knowledge of psychology. Often the fear is so great that one dares not admit it even to oneself.

—Carl Jung

OVER THE NEXT couple years we had ups and downs—there were times we almost broke up, issues with past romantic interests, a trip to Europe, and lots of playful banter mixed with sincere conversations. She loved pumpkin spice lattes when they came out in the fall (her favorite season) so I started calling her "P-Spice" in our flirty text messages. That later turned into her calling me "G-Spice" and soon after we were best friends. In the spring of 2012, Rachel and I moved into an apartment in the Albany Park neighborhood of Chicago. The decision to move in together was complicated—though because neither of us were getting any younger and because she was hands down the best girl I had ever dated, it was not a difficult choice.

That day in May when we signed the lease she was very excited. The apartment was a great find—a modern one-bedroom located above a Starbucks with only one neighbor to our right, an older Cuban lady. The four apartment units located above were converted office space and in front of one of the windows, a small baby angel statue sat on a pillar, looking out over the parking lot below.

It was out of place for a tiny shopping plaza but it was so small nobody ever noticed, least of which were the apartment dwellers, whose blinds were usually closed to keep out the sight of the gigantic McDonald's sign next door.

We sat in Rachel's blue GM Saturn outside the apartment and waited for the leasing agent to finish the paperwork. The sun was shining and the weather was warm, with trees around us not quite in full bloom.

I looked away from Rachel out the window to my left and noticed the lamppost in front of the Starbucks across the street. It was engulfed in bushes, partly covering the stem.

"How come you're not excited about this?" she asked me. "It's a great place."

"I don't know," I said looking down after glancing at her. "I'm trying to be cautious—maybe I'm nervous about the paperwork. I don't trust all the stuff they put in those contracts. I had a bad experience with a landlord once."

"But this should be a milestone in our relationship, and you don't seem to care. You always seem to ruin important moments, because you never get excited—about anything!"

"I'm sorry," I told her.

Rachel cried for several seconds. She wiped away a tear and then got angry. I looked back at the lamppost, trying to avoid confrontation.

"How are we supposed to build this relationship if there's no highs, if everything is the same, ALL the time?" she asked while raising her voice.

"I don't know," I replied in a defensive tone. "I'll try harder next time."

"There is no trying harder. Either you are or you aren't!"

Our neighborhood was advertised as the most multicultural one in the city, and it truly was about as eclectic as they come. There was a Thai restaurant and a convenience store owned by a Middle-Eastern family just across the street. If I ever ran out of milk and didn't have time to go to the grocery store, I would always pop over to the Kedzie and Wilson Food store that had a big sign in English with smaller Arabic letters written underneath. Exotic products like cardamom spice, puck cream cheese, and dates lined the shelves along with everyday food items such as milk and bananas. The two most popular places to visit in our neighborhood were a hardware store owned by a short, cranky old man named Jay, and a Mexican ice-cream store called Fruityland. Both were located just around the corner from our spacious apartment.

Probably the most peculiar aspect of the neighborhood where trees lined each side of the street was the deranged, middle-aged man who would occasionally walk Kedzie or Wilson Avenue shouting nonsensical babble to himself for no apparent reason. You could hear him approaching or walking from a distance, and he often sounded like the Tasmanian Devil cartoon character. It was demonic sounding and frightening when you first heard it, but over time, you got used to the verbal assault—like getting used to hearing gunfire or traffic. His stream of consciousness and onslaught of sounds seemed to come from the depths of his soul and the only thing decipherable in his speech was his acidic, self-flagellating tone. He was a part of the community though, and perhaps reflected something back to the people who couldn't quite grasp his significance. When I looked out the window for the first time to see who it was, I never really saw his face, just a tall man with brownish, unkempt hair. His face was featureless as far as I could tell, and most people crossed to the other side of the street whenever he appeared.

When there was a hard day or whenever either Rachel or I didn't feel well, we typically bonded over a trip to a nearby frozen yogurt place called Yogurt Square. Usually our days would end with one of us practicing trumpet in our living room, while the other would be on their computer answering emails or doing mindless work tasks. One evening in late summer, just before the sun went down, I approached her to see what she was up to. The apartment was getting dark but one could still see the orange glow of the fading sun coming from the window in the back bedroom.

"So, how's it going?" I asked Rachel after practicing my trumpet.

"Oh, trying to get my music together for the audition coming up," she replied while sitting at the long, wood dining room table. "It's stressing me out cause they didn't specify what exact part of the excerpt they want to hear. Normally it's from letter *G* to the end, but for some reason they didn't say which part."

"Do you feel ready for the audition?" I asked from where I was seated on the couch.

"I probably need to do another list. Can I play a list for you? I mean, I feel like I'm ready, but usually there's something outside of my control that happens and screws everything up."

"What excerpt were you working on earlier?" I asked. "Was it Mahler? I think it scared Hershey."

"Yeah, Mahler Five. Oh, man. Did I ever tell you the story of my high school trumpet teacher's dog?"

"No, I don't think so."

"The dog hated when he played Mahler Five. It was the only excerpt. He would start playing it downstairs and you could hear this rustling upstairs where the dog slept. Meanwhile, the teacher is still playing 'Duh, Duh, Duh Duhhh' and the dog gets up and comes running down the stairs during the middle of the excerpt— 'Oww, Owww'—and the dog starts freaking out. Then, he goes and plays Petroushka, and the dog is fine," Rachel laughed as she told the story. "It's just Mahler Five, the dog just couldn't deal with it."

"That's funny," I said with a smile. The amusement I felt inside was palpable yet somehow also controlled—as if not all the feelings could surface above my thick exterior. "Do you want to play for me right now or tomorrow?" I asked.

"Probably tomorrow cause it's getting late. What do you want to do tonight?"

"Do you want to watch something?" I asked.

"There's nothing to watch," she said as she became gloomy with a dejected look. "I don't want to sit on the couch and get bored. It would be better if you got more excited about things. How come you're like that?"

"I don't know—I think if I get excited, I'll just end up being disappointed."

"That doesn't make sense. Why would you be disappointed?"

"That's just how it always seems to be—I get excited about something and then somehow jinx myself or I get overwhelmed. Hey, do you want to go to Yogurt Square?"

"That sounds amazing," Rachel replied with her eyes lighting up. "But you have to keep talking to me about jinxing yourself."

We lived ten minutes away from Yogurt Square by train and had to time the trip just right in order to make sure we left our apartment with enough time to catch the next train heading east. When we got onto the Brown Line at the Kedzie station, both of us were like kids again. There was only one other person in the brightly lit car. As we sat down next to each other on the plastic, metallic bench, the pressures and responsibilities of adulthood momentarily lifted and we could enjoy each other's company with the anticipation of the sweet prize awaiting us just two stops away.

"So why do you think you jinx yourself?" she asked me after we sat down. There was a faint odor of marijuana, though nobody on the train was smoking.

I sighed and tried to think of the best way to put it into words. "It just seems like the moments I've been excited about something, things don't work out."

"Like what? What are you referring to?" she asked. "Don't you know that anticipation is sometimes the best part?"

"Maybe with my career or a concert. Maybe relationships. I get my hopes up, and then it doesn't turn out the way I thought it would. It's like what I feel on the inside never matches what happens on the outside."

We continued to chat as our train approached the adjoining neighborhood called Lincoln Square. We got off the train and descended the stairs located a block away from the shop. When we finally entered the store we were greeted by an overly bright, cheerful, and somehow artificial atmosphere. On the right side of the room, several large pictures of fruit hung on the lime green walls. To the left, numerous dispensers of yogurt contained flavors like Georgia Peach, Red Velvet, Dutch Chocolate and Cookies n' Cream.

"Oooh, they also have peanut butter," Rachel said excitedly. "What kind are you going to get?" she asked me.

"I'm feeling the peach, mixed with a little strawberry."

"What? That sounds awful," she said jokingly. "You should try mixing the peanut butter with some of the chocolate. It's amazing." We sat down at a nearby plastic table and dug in.

"This place is very green," I said with a smile while looking at our surroundings.

"Yes, they're going for a cool look," she replied. "It doesn't quite fit in with the rest of Lincoln Square though."

"Hey, we're not in Lincoln Square—we're in *Yogurt Square*," I reminded her with a chuckle. Rachel laughed.

"They should put in a *Coffee Square* or maybe a *Beer Square* too," I said between bites.

"I know what you would like—they need a *Cookie Square*," she said with a big smile, indicating she understood my sweet tooth.

"Now you're talking." I replied.

When we got back home that night, we felt better. It was always nice to have a break from the grind, and usually those breaks would involve some kind of fast food or quick treat. Other great moments with Rachel were when we danced. She really liked dancing and when I get going, I consider myself to be an entertaining dancer. Dancing allows me to express how pop music can make me feel—soulful and sweet at the same time. I'll cut loose if it's social dancing at a party or event, but if it's more structured where there are steps involved, I usually get frustrated because I can't express myself. Rachel could dance to pretty much any song or style, whereas for me it was really any style but rock. To this day I still don't understand how people can dance to 80's or 90's pop music that has no soul.

When we danced together Rachel would light up the room and let loose. If I liked the music, I would do the same; and if it was dated R & B music or funk, Rachel would always get a kick out of my intense reaction—my groove that defied all expectations and logic. She loved to joke with me about my antiquated music tastes and needless to say, she wasn't a fan of the funk. But she would still dance with me while holding back a smile. In fact, she always smiled when we danced and had a grin from one side of her face to the other. She would never try to lead me and instead followed my every move with eager energy and constant enthusiasm. I, on the other hand, had a gleam in my eye because I finally found someone who enjoyed being with me. That's why I loved her. We glided smoothly on the floor despite sometimes being behind the beat or missing a step. Our style together also attracted attention, not that I ever caught people staring. Somehow, this attractive redhead with the red flags was my people.

If Rachel had her faults, I was guilty just the same. I really wasn't ready to settle down and she was increasingly pushing the subject the longer we dated. One sticky, early summer night in 2013, I was in downtown Chicago at a salsa club. By this time, about two years into the relationship, Rachel advocated moving in together and we settled into that Albany Park apartment, where the stairwell occasionally smelled like freshly baked bread since there was a Subway on the opposite corner of the Starbucks. Rachel tried working at the coffee shop for a brief month or two before music conflicted with her schedule and she quit. Every morning at 4 a.m., the store downstairs would open and be a hot spot of activity for the morning commuters needing a caffeine fix. People would come and go, meet for a chat, work on their computers, and all the while, Rachel and I would lead a tranquil, domestic life upstairs. I told Rachel I was playing at the salsa club that humid evening, but really, I was going there to meet another girl I also liked. It was probably the first time I chose deceitful behavior in our relationship, due to the fact that I thought I could hide it and also because of the rush of excitement it gave me.

Nacional 27 was crowded that night. There were so many people that dancing was limited, thus making it easier for me to dance without making some kind of misstep or mistake. When I walked further into the club, there were two large gold pillars in the middle of the dance floor and a sea of people. I searched for what seemed like an eternity but probably was fifteen minutes, and the girl appeared out of the fog of brightly colored clothing mixed with the sound of loud timbale drums. Unfortunately she was there with a friend, who made me a little anxious. I took a deep breath and told myself to play it cool. After some common chitchat, the conversation proved to be amicable without the usual cross-examination, so my body and mind became more relaxed. The girl I was there to see seemed happy to see me and we also seemed to have a connection. I was surprised and excited at the same time, since she was a very attractive girl from Colombia and also the kind of girl I felt my heart was leading me to. Since I passed the friend inspection and danced just enough to be able to tell we were physically compatible, I said to her:

"Let me drive you home. Let's get out of here."

"OK, great." she replied. "I drove in from out of town and don't know if I'm staying at my friend's tonight. Let's go to your place."

I immediately headed towards my apartment, but also drove there with a sense of panic. My mind raced and searched for possible ways out of the current dilemma. I wanted to take her back to my apartment, but also knew that I couldn't do that under the circumstances. As we got closer and closer, I didn't know what to say to her.

"Yeah, I don't think we can go in cause I have a roommate."

She was immediately confused but also smart enough to understand the situation. I didn't tell her about living with a girlfriend, but she intuitively understood the situation.

"OK," she said, a little disappointed. "Well, can you drive me to my friend's car? She's waiting for me."

"Yeah, sure." I drove her there wondering why I couldn't reconcile the two sides of my heart. One side told me she was someone I should be with. The other side told me that Rachel, the girl already living with me in the apartment, was someone I should be with. What I needed out of a relationship superseded what I wanted.

Despite having my own red flags in our relationship, Rachel and I got engaged. Our strong friendship continued to blossom and we were both happy to commit to being partners for the long-haul. I thought I was being romantic when I proposed at one of my gigs at a bar while my band played "Isn't She Lovely" by Stevie Wonder. I counted off the rhythm section, left the stage of the dimly lit restaurant, walked over to her, and popped the question as I got down on one knee. She accepted of course, and since we didn't know what to do next, we celebrated like kids: with a huge sundae. A month or so later she made me redo the proposal however, because it didn't fit what she had in mind. In the end, I reproposed at the softball field where we first met, and felt like I let her down—that I should have thought it through more and considered what she would have wanted. A sense of failure grew within. It always seemed like in order for her life to matter, she needed the love story to be told the right way; and I was usually getting the story wrong.

Soon, the topic of kids was upon us. Rachel was disappointed I didn't bring up the idea of having children very often or have a lot of thoughts on the subject. The truth was that I lived more or less day-to-day and it was hard for me to think about anything in the future and make plans. We both agreed we wanted kids, but past that there wasn't much progress. When the topic came up a month before getting married in July 2014, I must have expressed uncertainty or was noncommittal about the issue and she was deeply hurt. On that particular occasion, after some alcohol, she came into our music practice room and threw around the music stand.

"What's wrong with me?" she screamed as she clutched the stand in her right hand.

"Why don't you want to have children with me?" she said, this time with tears and a look of exasperation.

She raised the stand quickly and hit my electric keyboard with a loud thud. I backed up a few steps just to make sure her next attempt wasn't aimed for me. I was afraid and angry, but I probably was more confused than anything. How could she be so different than the person I thought I knew?

"Rachel, you just damaged the piano!" I blurted out after recovering from the shock and checking to see if the keyboard worked. It didn't. "What the hell? Can't we talk about this tomorrow, when you're not like this?"

"We already did talk and you made yourself clear," she replied. "Why do things always have to be on your time?" She stormed out of the room, leaving the stand lying face down on the floor as an unwitting accomplice.

When she left I was still a little in shock and didn't know what to do. Later that night, I sat down at the computer and sent an email to her brother. My hands hesitated at first, but the gnawing sense of worry pushed me forward.

Hello James, I don't have your phone # and I need to talk to you about Rachel. Please forward me your number and I'll try to give you a call tomorrow when you have time.

I woke up the next day to his email reply and was prepared to call him back. But Rachel found out and was offended that I would call him and betray her like that. He wasn't someone she even had a close relationship with anymore and didn't see him as someone to confide in. In the end, I never did make that call. The other side of her remained partially hidden and never discussed with the outside world. I could say the same thing for my other side.

Eventually, living together created more friction between us and we would argue about doing chores or paying bills. A week after her brother's email reply I sat at the long wood table doing work on my computer. My back was towards Rachel, who was on the couch watching something on TV.

"I need someone to help me get more gigs," I said out loud with my face buried in the computer, typing an email.

"You're not good at networking. You need to talk more to people before and after your gigs," she said matter-of-factly. "I don't want you to take this the wrong way, but I wish I could be in your shoes 'cause I would be so much better at it." She had a satisfied look on her face and while she spoke in a non-hostile way, it was direct and intended to give me a jolt. Rachel could press buttons if she wanted to and this was one of those times. My anger started to boil up from underneath. "Can you please shut up?" I snapped back at her, emphasizing the last two words. There was a short silence.

"Why can't you be more personable at your gigs?" she replied, ignoring my statement. It was clear she was going to move past the stop sign.

I was angry and it felt like steam was starting to come out of my ears. I picked up my laptop and slammed it down on the table. She immediately took notice and there was a brief silence in the room. "Why did you do that?" she asked when some time had passed.

"Leave me alone. I think I just broke it," I said. I had knocked the hard drive loose and would have to get a new laptop. Other times wine glasses broke, and then there was the blender. Another time she learned from me, and took the water filter pitcher and slammed it into the sink. Things breaking in the kitchen happened enough that our dog Hershey would later become traumatized by the sound and would never like the sound of dishes being put away in the kitchen, or any kitchen noise louder than normal. I later learned to not break things, and my strategy became walking away or disengaging. This seemed to work until she accused me of stonewalling. When you spend so much time apart from your emotions, it's hard to deal with them when they arise. Both of us needed better coping strategies.

Chapter 5
Layers

Disguised since childhood,
haphazardly assembled
From voices and fears and little pleasures,
we come of age as masks.
Our true face never speaks.

—Rainer Maria Rilke, Poet

IN BUDDHISM THEY say there are seven veils of illusion and that removing each veil increases one's enlightenment. The journey I was on at that time seemed clouded by illusions, like things were just beyond my grasp or distorted enough to elude my full comprehension.

As far as my appearance: I had a full head of brown hair, which sat nicely on my slender, tall, six-foot frame. I was attractive in a nice, pleasant way, though not really sure how much. I was more introverted than extroverted, more bookish or rigid than spontaneous, and more of a follower than a leader. Rachel made me take one of those personality tests once and I came out as an INTJ, which stands for "Introversion, Intuition, Thinking, Judging". I liked the arts, but wasn't huge into the arts. I liked sports, but preferred not to be a die-hard fan. I enjoyed Latin culture and speaking Spanish, but I'm white and felt too reserved to fit in. I liked playing music, but never seemed to be able to do it as a full-time job. I really liked jazz music, but didn't consider myself to be a hard-core jazz nerd. I enjoyed studying psychology and intellectual topics, but never went full throttle into that realm either. I never seemed to camp out in one specific area for too long, which kept me from feeling grounded or like I fit in. That seemed to be one constant in my life—that I was like some kind of imposter, trying on layer after layer until I got the fit just right.

With Rachel, I presented different sides slowly and she was always willing to know more. She had the patience to gradually peel back layers, and that's why I could share things with her I probably couldn't share with others. One night in 2014, while still living in our Albany Park apartment, we sat down to watch an episode of *Breaking Bad*.

She had been trying to get me to watch *Breaking Bad* with her ever since she started the series during her time off on a work trip to Scotland. It was the first show we watched and enjoyed together. The long white couch we sat on used to be her parents', and was cleverly disguised with a beige couch cover that hid its previous use.

"Just watch the first episode with me. I promise you'll like it. It has a lot of action and crazy plot twists," she said.

"What's it about?" I asked her.

"Well, there's this high school teacher who gets into selling meth 'cause he has cancer."

"It's a crime show about selling drugs?"

"No, you just have to watch it. It's like, he has kind of a dual life and his wife doesn't know but suspects something is up."

I wrapped my arm around her shoulder while watching, and her head became nestled against my chest. We had never been closer as a couple as that night, when we bonded over a common interest. As we watched, I became hooked. The show was as addictive as the meth Walter White cooked up nearly every episode. It wasn't like other shows that developed the characters before the action. This was the other way around, where the action and drama told the story of the characters. When we finished the first episode, I turned to Rachel and said:

"That was crazy. That guy White is clearly not cut out to be doing what he's doing and somehow, things worked out."

"Oh, just wait. They get even better," she replied. "Want to watch another one?" she asked with eager anticipation.

"Sure. We got time."

"Do you think you have a hidden side to you?" she asked me while glancing back and looking over her shoulder.

"Well, I am a Gemini. But I'm not nearly as messed up as Walter White."

"Can you imagine being a high school teacher and trying to sell drugs?"

"No. Knowing me, if I did something like that I would immediately get caught."

She turned around abruptly and laughed. "Why's that?"

"Well, don't you remember what I told you once before? I was arrested one time for doing something stupid in college—not thinking straight at a party, typical young person stuff, taking beer from someone's apartment without permission."

Her eyes searched the room for the memory. "Oh, wow. Yeah, I forgot."

"The charges were later dismissed, but it definitely traumatized me for the next ten years."

When she complained years later that I needed to open up more to her, I was confused. I had already shared more with her than anybody else I had ever known. I told her about my childhood fears and my general insecurities. She even visited my childhood home and met most of my closest friends from throughout my life. What else was there to share?

Another thing I previously revealed to Rachel was when I suffered a nervous breakdown while in graduate school in Texas. The turning point came when I drove home late one night, collapsed on my kitchen floor and cried uncontrollably. I had gone to a jam session that evening in Fort Worth at a place called the Black Dog Tavern. One walked down some stairs to enter the club and even though the lighting was dim, I swore I once saw the actor Morgan

Freeman at a table by himself reading a book. On that particular evening though, I drank vodka sodas all night, since I had developed a habit of drinking gin or vodka and pretending it was just water to conceal that I was consuming alcohol. I was hyper aware of my surroundings, like a lab rat getting used to its cage. After one too many that night, I ended up hitting on a younger girl and we went back to her car and sat inside. We fooled around a little and she soon scared me senseless by informing me her dad was a cop— implying that she could call him at any time if I was out of line. All of a sudden I thought twice about what I had gotten myself into and immediately left. I was so scared that cops were going to follow me back home and arrest me again that I hid in my apartment and broke down from the pressure. The shame and guilt of getting arrested the first time in college still clung to me like the Texas heat one could not escape.

Not long after first arriving in Texas, I had developed a quasi-schizophrenic outlook on life and later could no longer bear the weight of the world-view I had constructed. The stress and anxiety of adjusting to a new chapter in my life and trying to fit in caused me to reimagine what reality presented me. During that period in my life, I kept a journal. I wrote about new meanings of different colors and numbers, or at least new ways I interpreted them. For example, I sometimes wore red shirts to signify I was wounded or bleeding. It was like my soul was bleeding, or perhaps that I was a wounded angel. I wrote about how I felt like people were out to get me. Usually this feeling coincided with when I drove on the highway or drove late at night. I also had a strange anxiety after going to a church, which myself and another trumpet player attended for several months. I sent a bizarre letter to the church saying I could no longer be a member, and somehow the other trumpet player later got cancer and ended up passing away within a year or so.

I always looked for a shortcut or a magic phrase to make life easier and desperately tried to find relief from my nerves. In some ways I blamed the state of Texas. In other ways, I blamed myself. I guess going from the state of Washington to graduate school in a college town north of Dallas was too much culture shock for me. It didn't help that I had social anxiety issues that surfaced during my beginning college years, later resulting in depression. I just wasn't able to adapt to a new school, new friends, and a totally new "Texas" way of life.

Other things that happened then I don't remember well because I burned the journal out of shame. It was a period in my life (I was twenty-four years old at the time) when my brain tried to find a shortcut or figure out how life worked. When it all became too much for me to handle, I stopped. I vowed to never go down that path again. I was creative enough to imagine things that might have been partially true, but really had no basis in reality. I never told anybody my thoughts because I knew they sounded crazy—I was living an intense pseudo-reality as a sort of life experiment, and that could only last so long. By the time I met Rachel years later, I no longer had issues or schizophrenic thoughts. I had built a stronger framework over past emotional setbacks and moved past that turbulent time in my life. But I was still like an ugly duckling afraid of its shadow—if only because it loomed so large in the background.

Around the same time we watched *Breaking Bad* that year, Rachel and I agreed to do a presentation for a kid's television program that the Peoria Symphony had arranged. They taped the program in front of a live audience, and previous segments usually featured musicians from the orchestra. Since Rachel worked regularly with the ensemble, she had helped get us the gig. Our presentation consisted of introducing the trumpet to a novice audience and showing how the instrument sounded in different styles of music. It was a good example of us working together musically because we typically played and worked in separate groups—for her, classical; for me, jazz. The presentation was also a litmus test, in a way, for our relationship in general, documenting how we would work together under pressure and if we could successfully put on a good show.

The program was recorded in a dark backstage area. There was a small but respectable audience there, with kids seated in front and a mixture of parents and random adults in the back. Both of us were a little nervous since we had never presented anything like that before. We prepared for the engagement by coming up with a detailed outline of what we would say and play, and ran through the presentation once or twice at home.

That Sunday afternoon in February, we both wore black: Rachel, a black pantsuit, and me, a black sweater and gray slacks. Her silver trumpet contrasted slightly with my gold one, and we opened up the program with a fanfare I had written for the occasion, bells pointing in the direction of a large microphone. With music and our program notes on music stands in front of us, we talked about the instrument, all the while standing in front of a navy-blue background similar to a green screen. We discussed how the trumpet works, its history, and how it sounds in different styles of music.

"Where does sound come from?" Rachel asked the children in front, giving them a big warm smile and exuding an abundance of positive energy.

At first, the kids didn't know what to say or how to respond.

"Put your hand on your throat and say 'Ahh'," she continued. "What do you feel?"

"It's moving, kind of vibrating," one kid said.

"Yes! Vibration. That is your vocal cords vibrating together to make a sound. This is how you're able to talk and sing. We need a vibration to make a sound on our trumpets, but since we don't talk or sing through our instrument, we need to find another way to make a vibration. Can everyone move their hand from their throat to their lips and do this with me?" Rachel flubbed her lips together to make a crude vibrating noise. Some kids giggled. After she showed how the lips could also vibrate into a tiny metal mouthpiece, I delved into the history.

"When the trumpet was invented, it was limited in what it could play...Later on as these buttons were added, it could start to play more melodies," I stated in a confident manner, hiding my nerves. I played a part of the Haydn Trumpet Sonata to demonstrate.

Our presentation was off to a good start. The children watched and listened intently with their eyes fixated on the two contrasting images in front of them—an over-confident girl with red hair and an under-confident guy with brown hair. Our program demonstrated ornamentation and how, with three new keys or valves, the trumpet could now not only play melodies but also embellish them. I played the first part of Trumpet Voluntary, a stately song usually played at weddings when the bride walks down the aisle. Next, Rachel demonstrated the same part, with ornamentation. She moved up, down, and around the notes to show the dexterous ability of the horn. The metal valves clicked with a sense of assured finality.

Then, as I started to play the next part of the song, my mind went blank. It was as if someone pulled the plug and there was just an emptiness inside my head. Rachel looked at me with a confused face. Although I practiced and knew the song, I hadn't played it enough for it to be automatic. Normally in those circumstances, I just gave myself a minute to recall the song—when you're taping a TV show, that's harder to do. They told us ahead of time that we could stop and take a time out if need be, and they would edit out the stopping and starting. Breaking from our prepared schtick, I spoke to someone beyond the lights.

"Uh, yeah. Can we stop?" I asked nervously. Our flow was broken. Rachel seemed disappointed, and her voice wavered a little as she tried to pick up the slack and continue with the next part of our presentation. We were doing such a good job of being in character, but another part of myself intruded. It felt kind of like tripping myself, though I didn't understand how or why that would happen.

We continued on fairly well with the rest of the program, though my sense of failure for messing up was omnipresent afterwards, and I apologized to Rachel and the people recording the TV show. They assured me that it wouldn't be an issue. Later on, we found out that the orchestra didn't end up using our program after all. We never found out what happened to the footage of that day because Peoria kept that kind of stuff under lock and key for some reason.

Things like that had a way of happening when Rachel and I did certain things together. When we went on hikes, we often got lost, with me leading and thinking I knew the way, only to get confused if I made a misstep or read the map wrong. It's probably partly why Rachel used to say we just weren't on the same page. The one thing I knew deep down was that there was another side that seemed to sabotage these situations. While most people would consider slight mishaps to be normal, I had a suspicion that there was more to it than that.

Chapter 6
Rachel, Part One

Jung has said that to be in a situation where there is no way out, or to be in a conflict where there is no solution, is the classical beginning of the process of individuation. It is meant to be a situation without solution...But if he (man) is ethical enough to suffer to the core of his personality, then generally because of the insolubility of the conscious situation, the Self manifests.

—Marie-Louise von Franz, Psychologist

RACHEL HAD A wonderful sense of humor. She used to joke with me that she knew "how you are going to go when your time comes." I was often clumsy and unco-ordinated when putting on pants in the morning, to the point where I sometimes almost fell over. Each time she witnessed this, she would laugh at me and make her remark.

When she was out at a bar or at a social function, Rachel enjoyed showing people how one of her pinky fingers was sub-stantially smaller than it should have been. She liked connecting with people by comparing hands and proving that indeed, she had a unique pinky. She also kept an arsenal of "that's what she said" jokes on hand for those moments when she could slip in a funny or just break the ice. With my family, at least, she was always able to find the humor in the moment and make us laugh at just the right time. On one trip to San Diego with my family, we'd had the misfortune of watching my family's alma mater play against the University of Minnesota in the Holiday Bowl. The game was probably the worst football game I've ever seen—as if the objective of the game had changed to who could play worse and who was most inept. When we all went to a bar afterwards in the Gaslamp district to forget about what we just experienced, Rachel somehow got the idea that my seventy-year-old father should do an "Irish car bomb," which is a shot of whiskey dropped into a pint of Guinness. It turned out to be the highlight of the day, really. My dad laughed, everyone at the table smiled, and at least for a moment we were able to forget about the stupid game.

Another thing I did that would make Rachel laugh was say the word "chocolate." I think somewhere along the line, I picked up a Bill Cosby-like way of pronouncing the word and every time—and I do mean every time—I said the word, she would repeat it using my inflection. At first I was sensitive to the fact that she thought it was hilarious, and over the years I would try to avoid saying the word or change my pronunciation so she couldn't pounce on me with her repetition of it. Overall, I was fine with it though, and it became a running joke between us. She was always pretty good at picking up people's idiosyncrasies and finding the humor in them. Anytime someone made a funny noise or sound in a story they were telling, Rachel would latch on to that and make them repeat it. "Wait, how did that go again?" she would say with a laugh or smile.

A week or so after we taped the kids' program in Peoria, we had another gig to go back for—a Valentine's Day concert with the orchestra. Once again, Rachel had used her influence to get me a job as composer, arranger, and performer. I provided arrangements for the orchestra, backed up two singers in a Pops concert, and my own jazz group was going to perform one of my original compositions with the orchestra. It was a dream job really, and it was all thanks to Rachel.

We drove to Peoria together that cold, icy day in February, and a snowstorm made driving treacherous, with wind and snow reducing visibility to a minimum. An uneasy feeling sat inside my stomach because I knew there was a battle going on between my expectations for the concert and the fear that Rachel and I, or perhaps the rest of the band, would not make it. The reality of being a musician in Chicago was that it was normal for band members to cancel at the last second or not be available for a low-paying gig when they had the opportunity to get paid more somewhere else. Experiencing that time after time had worn down my hopes and forced me to live in a world of caring less, essentially protecting myself from future disappointment. Maybe we would have to play the concert without all the band—maybe we would get stuck ourselves and be late. I tried to remain calm and thought that if I downplayed everything, I could reach an equilibrium. As snow whipped around our car, I grasped the steering wheel tightly, kept my gaze ahead, and didn't waste any excess energy on conversation. In those kinds of journeys, even the person next to you focuses on just arriving safely. At some point the feeling of dread sank deep into my body, to the point where it was uncomfortable to do anything but concentrate. The roads were not slippery, but the fear came from the possibility of losing control and sliding into the unforgiving white mess on either side. At one point, a big gust of wind and snow hit the car and pushed it enough that I had to fight back with the steering wheel. A tense foreboding gripped me for about an hour. Eventually, a city appeared in the distance and the uneasiness subsided a little. After we miraculously arrived, the other members of the band also appeared—luckily, they somehow got there without a hitch.

I later stood backstage at the large performing arts theater before my turn to perform and listened to the orchestra play an arrangement of a Billy Joel song. Rachel was sitting in the trumpet section and, from my position at stage left, she was easy to spot, with her fiery red hair and poised demeanor. She had a solo on the melody of "Just The Way You Are," and it was the first time I was able to listen to her sound. Normally when I went to her orchestra concerts, it was always hard to hear her apart from the ensemble, though I was never sure why.

Her sound was pure, bold, and inspiring—so distinct that you had to listen to it. It drew you near to her because that was what she wanted—she wanted the warmth of people around her and the connection that came from people listening to her express herself through music. It was also the first time I had really heard the true self behind the Rachel I had known up to that point. She hadn't yet lost part of her innocence, as people are apt to do when they get older. Her round, fluffy sound was both direct and poignant. It had a noble quality because she had sincere expectations of life that came from the heart, and you could hear that in her playing. As I listened, her sound drew me in and I felt a strange comforting feeling. Her sound wrapped around my body and my head cocked to one side as I listened. It was as if, in revealing herself to me for the first time, she was asking me to accept her. When I later tried to get a recording of the performance to remember the event, the administration of the orchestra was not forthcoming for some strange reason. After the concert that evening, I spoke to her:

"I liked your solo on the Billy Joel song. I could really hear you."

"Oh, thanks. It wasn't that great, was it?" she said, seemingly embarrassed.

"Yeah, I liked it," I replied.

"Well, thank you. I normally don't like to play solos like that. I was a little nervous when I played," she said.

Rachel was courageous. When she was a teenager, she attended a baseball camp with her brother and was the only girl amongst a hundred other boys. That didn't mean she didn't have nerves, however, and so later during her music career she took beta-blockers (pills that reduce the heart rate and lessen anxiety) for almost all of her performances, including rehearsals. Even then, she would frequently be a wreck before she played. "It doesn't matter if I'm performing in front of kindergartners or if it's my peers—I still get nervous," she used to tell me.

It was something you probably wouldn't have recognized in the audience because she usually performed so well. Her recital repertoire was like an Olympic performance because she frequently chose difficult pieces to prove her amazing talent. Through her musical training, Rachel learned to manage her stress. It also most likely helped her to regulate the intense emotions she felt. In the end though, the stress and anxiety performing caused her was probably one of the reasons she wanted to eventually end up with a different career. In fact, she probably would have made a good couples counselor, and talked about going back to school to be a therapist of some kind. By the time she got the job in academia, she didn't have as much time to pursue that option.

Her dual combination of strength and fragility was something I could relate to and one reason why I made a lot of sacrifices to try to get close to her. There was the time I procured lots of classical CDs, and spent hours listening and marking specific spots to assist her with one of her orchestral auditions. There was the time I handed over my trumpet students to her and helped her find work at a nearby private school. There was the time I came over to her Rogers Park apartment and spent an entire day doing her taxes. On my birthday that year, she gave me a touching card with two golden retrievers looking at each other on the front that read: "You're my favorite person in the world..." and inside was a typed letter:

Greg, You are probably wondering why I am giving you the same card that I gave you for Valentine's Day and the reason is quite simple...because this card so perfectly articulates my feelings about you. You really are my favorite person in the world, the one I love to go new places with, talk to and hang out with...you are my best friend and I love you completely with all my heart!

Our love story has forever changed me and helped me to grow in more ways than I will ever be able to tell you. I had no idea, from the first moment I met you, that we would spend the rest of our lives together, and I am grateful for that! Love is not a fairy tale or something that is obsessive or blinding. Love is real and deep to the core and grows throughout time.

You have taught me what "true love" is. It is a love that lasts through "the good, the bad, and the ugly." Love is a choice, and is unconditional and forgiving. Opening my eyes to this and being patient with me in the process is a blessing and a gift. Thank you for truly being the love of my life, my best friend and my soon to be partner in life!

I love you always, Rachel

On her thirtieth birthday, I tried to return the favor and wrote her a note that explained why she was special to me. Written inside a blank Hallmark card of four puppies carrying a stick, I handwrote a note in black ink:

You're special because you're:

a red panda, you have a good sense of humor, you're sweet, generous, easy going, cute, you play good orchestral trumpet, like sports, you laugh at my jokes, think I'm funny, you have a long tongue, cook well, love dogs, you are a dog, put up with my unique non-communicative way of being, and you find me attractive.

But most importantly, you're special because you have my heart. Love, Greg

Chapter 7
Rachel, Part Two

It is only with the heart that one can see rightly; what is essential is invisible to the eye.
                    —Antoine de Saint-Exupéry, Writer

THANKSGIVING WAS HER favorite holiday, and so we routinely spent that time with her family in the suburbs of Minneapolis. I enjoyed visits to her family home because it was such a warm and inviting place. The house was a traditional three-bedroom. It was cozy, not spacious, and if you looked around, you could see knick-knacks, family photos, and trophies of musical and sports achievements. My favorite place in the house was the basement where there was a baby grand piano that I would occasionally play for fun. In fact, the basement was the center of activity for many years during Rachel's childhood, since that was also the place where her mother and father taught thousands of private lessons for piano, clarinet, and trumpet. When you walked downstairs you were greeted by a large basket of candy and snacks, rewards for students who came to the lesson prepared. Also in the basement was a tackboard plastered with family photographs of Rachel and her brother. The photos I loved most were those of Rachel hugging the family dog—there was probably nothing that brought out joy in her face and eyes more than being with her trusted companions. In one photo, her face is lit up with a big smile and her eyes twinkle as she wraps her arms around a young cocker spaniel named Buffy. The reaction she had around dogs was still very much the same when I first met her; whenever she saw one, she would shout "Puppy!" and rush to try and meet the new furry friend. The other photos I enjoyed were from junior high—mainly because you could start to see the blend of her younger self with her adult self. A more slender, sleek Rachel started to display some of the beautiful characteristics in her face reminiscent of her Russian/Slavic family background—piercing, expressive eyes; resplendent lips; fair skin; and an oval-shaped face.

During Thanksgiving that year, Rachel was excited to go home, eat good food, and visit with her parents, brother's family, cousins, and aunts and uncles. Her traditional tasks during the holiday included peeling potatoes and apples, and making a broccoli casserole that everyone raved about. She loved helping her mom in the kitchen and enlisted me to help her as well—that way, everyone got to spend quality time together.

The other aspect of Thanksgiving that stood out was that Rachel felt anxious that I would get bored. It wasn't my family after all, and it wasn't my hometown. On at least one occasion I did get bored and spent an hour or so in the basement rewatching old VHS tapes of the Minnesota Twins in the World Series. Some other day, not long after peeling and coring apples in the kitchen, she said to me:

"What do you want to do? I feel bad if you're too bored." The clock located above the stairs from the entryway struck 12 p.m. and played a part of Beethoven's "Ode to Joy".

"I don't know. Can we visit the General Mills factory and get free cereal samples?" I replied.

"I'm not sure. I don't think that really exists."

"Why? Isn't General Mills where they make the cereal? Like, can't you see where they make Cocoa Puffs?"

"They don't do that anymore. Do you want to go to a basketball game?"

"Maybe, we can check who's playing," I said.

"Oh," she said, pondering something. "I don't really know if I can do Black Friday this year with my mom."

"Why?"

"Well, do you want to go? I'd rather spend time with you."

"Well how long you gonna be? If it's not too long, it shouldn't be bad. Maybe we can meet up afterwards."

"Yeah, that might work," she said in a happy tone. "You can just hang out with my dad at home. We'll text you when we're ready and we can all meet up for lunch."

During that vacation trip I became acquainted with the Super Moon buffet and the Sunshine Factory Bar and Grill—both local favorites. I also heard unique family stories about her diabetic father, energetic mother, and religious brother. There was the time Rachel had to drive to a McDonald's miles away because her father had gone too far on his jogging route while training for a marathon. There was the time her mother drove through the night down to a music festival in North Carolina and later had to confront the music director in order to get her daughter the opportunity to play the right part in the orchestra. There was the time her brother went to live in Mexico and came back with a young wife, who got hit by a car and later fled back to her family and was never heard from again. Her mother also told me the story about young, effervescent Rachel. She was a fun, bubbly kid who exuded a lot of joy, and it was common around the house to see this fearless, witty child frequently playing her violin (her first instrument) in front of people, with spurts of giggling mixed in with the music. If denied in her search for connection, her search to coalesce, she found extreme ways to protest. Around the time she was in kindergarten, her mother told her she was going on a trip to visit her grandma in Arizona and would have to miss school. Instead of being excited, Rachel was upset she wouldn't get to see her friends and classmates. While her mom taught a music lesson nearby, she cut out pictures of those friends to take with her. The scissors made a snipping sound that matched her contempt—each face carefully extracted from the school picture and placed in her front pocket. Just for spite, she also cut the cords to the electric blanket underneath her. It started with a few innocent snips and proceeded to a more definitive slice that left no doubt of her intentions. Fortunately, she cut the right cords and avoided any harm.

I listened with great interest and curiosity to each story and slowly learned to be part of their family—one that was about as nice and supportive as they come. The part I would play in their continued family history was still undetermined.

After going to lunch at a shopping mall a couple towns over, we came back to her home and played with the family dogs, Coda and Gus. We let them out in their backyard, adjacent to a huge field, and at one point I made a dramatic run to Coda and embraced him like we were long-lost pals. The run and embrace felt liberating, like a breath of fresh air. It also seemed a little out of place, like I was putting on a show. Coda was a happy-go-lucky golden retriever and might as well have been Rachel's spirit animal. The joy on his face was so infectious that part of his spirit passed on to me and I couldn't help but try to match his joy. Rachel laughed in the background at my over-the-top performance. She had the ability to channel her inner Coda, and so her face could also light up when she saw me or when we went out on a date. Dating someone like her didn't always go smoothly, but what was easy was how much energy and emotion she gave you, and that's partly what drew me to her.

When we came back inside, the little salt-and-pepper terrier named Gus ran over and jumped on top of the couch to look outside. The large dining room window had an impressive view of the backyard and large field that we had just left. The dog peered out into the field with great interest because something had caught his attention. It darted back and forth near the edge of the field, where there was a small wooded area. Rachel hurried to the window.

"Oh, look!" she said. "It's the fox." Her excitement and curiosity almost matched the dog's. The medium-sized red animal made his appearance that afternoon, and it temporarily became the show. Rachel's face lit up, and she became caught up in the drama of where the fox was going and what the fox was doing.

"You should come look quick, before he disappears," she told me. I meandered over to the couch where she had propped herself up, and peered over the back. I couldn't match her excitement level and desperately wanted to know how such an event could stir up her adrenaline. I'll admit it was mildly interesting to see an animal as graceful and adroit as the fox pass by the house, but I still was at a loss as to the greater significance for Rachel. By the time I made it to the window, the fox had disappeared into the woods.

"Where did the fox go?" she asked Gus in a melodramatic voice while rubbing his ears.

The fox made an appearance almost on each visit for a little while. I only saw it once but never got a clear view. One really never saw the face of the fox—just its long, thin body as it glided through the field like floating through air. Just when you thought it might stick around for a while to be seen, it was gone.

After the show was over, we went over to the dining room to help prepare for dinner. Rachel showed me the bottle of Manischewitz located in an ornate hutch containing wine glasses, and pointed to the bottle at the bottom.

"Have you ever tried Manischewitz?" she asked.

"No, why?"

"That stuff is awful. My parents don't really drink, but they'll occasionally bust that out for Seder or another holiday," she said. "You should try some if you never had it."

I considered the invitation for a brief moment. "Maybe later," I replied. I wondered why her parents didn't drink—and if they didn't drink, why did Rachel? Why did alcohol affect her like it did?

While I couldn't understand her drinking issue, what I did relate to was the concept of jinxing oneself. I understood what it was like to be overwhelmed by a moment or to be caught in an event that seemed larger than myself—like the pseudo-schizophrenic time in Texas, or the children's program in Peoria. That was the other connection that drew us together, because while I had been running away from those moments my whole life out of fear, Rachel showed me what it was like to dive in headfirst—I was in awe of her courage. It often seemed like running into a fire despite knowing one would get burnt. The baggage we both inherited was similar somehow, like we were both unknowingly fighting the subconscious battles of our parents, or perhaps dealing with a shadow larger than life. When something seems like it's holding you back, you have two options: resign to your fate or fight it. She chose the latter.

Chapter 8
Faults and Transgressions

If you bring forth that which is within you, what you bring forth will save you. If you do not bring forth that which is within you, what you do not bring forth will destroy you.
                                                    —Gospel of Thomas

To say I resigned myself to my own fate would not be an accurate description because of ways I found to work around the situation at hand. In matters of the heart, I was foolish and immature. Somehow, the learning of a language became intertwined with romance—like two tree branches wrapping around and around until they fused together.

If you are trying to learn a language, it is important to practice speaking with a native-speaker one-on-one or in a group and, for me, I found the best way to do that was to meet online, Spanish-speaking girls learning English, and then go chat in a café and have a language exchange. I first became interested in learning Spanish while in college, since it provided an intellectual challenge and I needed the language credit to graduate. I also had a crush on my Spanish professor, so I would be lying if I said there wasn't something about the women that lured me to it as well. Throughout the years, the cultural exploration of learning another language gave me another outlet for expression and another way of looking at the world. The exotic and foreign nature of Spanish culture attracted me right away, when I really heard salsa music for the first time on my trip to Miami while working as a musician on a cruise ship—it seemed like such a light and carefree outlook on life, in stark contrast to my own.

The language exchanges were always more interesting with girls, and it seemed like they were also more beneficial. It was selfish of me, because although these were not even people I'd call friends, on occasion I would push things and try to make more of the relationship. This included going to a movie or hanging out at a bar. The encounters took place in Chicago shortly before 2014, and were also something I didn't tell Rachel anything about. When she found out, it almost ended our engagement. I told her it should be possible to have friends of the opposite sex, and in many ways that's true. But I think she knew better. She understood that sometimes there could be a dual motive and that I was trying to maintain my single ways. I told her I wouldn't go down that path again if it affected her that much. For some reason though, I returned to a tactic I had learned when I was younger. I vowed to keep that part of myself more hidden, more secret, and buried that part of myself underneath all of those other layers. Unable to express my true desire, I wrapped it up and banished it below.

I kept secret that I continued to meet and chat in Spanish with girls at coffee shops, even after being married in 2014. I figured if there's no harm, there's no foul, and if it was kept out of the way, there could be no detriment. It was part of my job requirement to be proficient at speaking Spanish, after all, and if I didn't get better at it, I couldn't get a job. Most of these encounters (probably around five over a three-year period) were just casual chats in a coffee shop, and nothing more. But on two separate occasions in 2015 and 2017, I pushed the relationship further—I tried to keep part of my heart separate from Rachel and thought I could somehow maintain a hidden dual existence. I was running and hiding from myself, but also not quite knowing who that self really was. The irony was that I knew what I was doing was wrong, and it required a lot of effort to carry out. Yet I chose to cross the line just the same and often wondered why I was jinxing myself or getting carried away by a feeling within. It was as if the two tree branches I mentioned before crossed many times and then eventually created a split, a crack that revealed the true direction of the other.

Prior to meeting Rachel, usually my relationships with girls reminded me of when Lucy pulls the football away from Charlie Brown as he tries to kick it. I was always trying hard but falling flat on my face. Rachel, however, wasn't like that. She wouldn't pull the football away. In fact, if anything, she would help me kick the ball. Consequently, I knew she was somebody I should be with long-term. The problem was that by the time I met her, my heart was pulling me in a different direction. It seemed there were two types of love. One type of love was a passionate, caring relationship with a girl who spoke Spanish. I equated Latin culture with affection and compassion, and saw it as a way to fill a void in my own life. Another type of love was more platonic and supportive—the kind of love I felt for Rachel. The same duality of platonic-versus-romantic love, evident in Federico García Lorca's play entitled *Bodas de sangre,* was present, and I could not come to terms with either. The play features a woman torn between two lovers, who ends up choosing one yet secretly desiring the other. The two lovers confront each other in battle and both die, leaving the woman desolate and without purpose in life. Just like the woman, I didn't realize my heart would continue to seek the passionate kind of love with someone else, nor did I realize that I could have also had that with Rachel if I had known how to get to the core of who I am. In retrospect, I suspect that Rachel also played a small part in this relationship dynamic because, while she would never pull the football out from under me, her own self-destructive behavior and porcupine-style love definitely had a distancing effect.

It seemed like I was making a mature decision in later deciding to settle down and marry Rachel, and was pleased to do so. I also was willing to make a lot of sacrifices because I didn't think marriage would happen for me otherwise. Some of the negative sides to her personality could overshadow the positive sides, but I thought that's how life was. You take the good with the bad. Wasn't

I the same way, after all? The drawback was that the negative sides made it difficult for me to fall madly in love with her. I loved her, but it wasn't the intense, head-over-heels kind of love she desperately craved. She wanted to be cherished and adored, but it wasn't something I was good at. I could be very thoughtful and loving in a supportive kind of way, but romance, on the other hand, was something that I couldn't access very well because I was always making do with what life gave me. Romance became a casualty in the battle between my aspirations and reality—between feelings of hope and excitement and despair. I could never quite match up what I felt on the inside with what was happening on the outside.

For Rachel, it wasn't necessarily an ideal relationship, but she thought it could be improved and regarded my commitment with gratitude. She still sought the moment when I would fall madly in love with her. She tried cooking elaborate recipes, wearing sexy dresses, and continued to display her musical prowess. I didn't change though, and nothing seemed to get the reaction she wanted. The busier I became with work, the more I buried the emotions that I could only express through music and not with her. I suppose it's common for some couples to retreat into their separate camps after marriage and, while I never withdrew from Rachel that much, there was something I wasn't ready to uncover. I married her in part so she could draw something out of me and help confront a part of my unknown face. I just wasn't ready and in many ways, she wasn't either.

Chapter 9
Trauma

The distorting mirrors…are created in the acute suffering of trauma, but, once established, they perpetuate suffering—a chronic, tolerable form of it.

—Donald Kalsched, Psychologist

THE NEXT TWO years of our lives consisted of normal married life. Rachel explored different career options and went back to school to get a nursing certificate. I also went back to school and got a K-12 teaching certificate. The highlight of those years was when she interviewed for the music teaching position in Virginia and passed with flying colors. By June of 2017, we had already moved there for her job at the university, but I returned to Chicago that month for a couple performances with my band. Since I'm also an avid reader and admirer of the Swiss psychologist Carl Jung, I paid a visit to the Jung Institute for a workshop. I arrived downtown and entered the building of the Institute with anticipation and a little bit of nerves. It was a sixteen-story brown skyscraper, sleekly sculpted with a fancy cafeteria on the ground floor. The workshop I signed up for, the only one available that day, was on trauma and art therapy. I honestly didn't know what I was getting myself into—all I knew was that I wanted to visit the Institute and participate in a workshop to learn more about Jung. It was the first time I had ever participated in something that I previously had only read about in books.

I took the elevator up to the fourth floor, wandered the hall-way, passed a small, ornate library and followed the sound of voices into a large conference room. An older lady with white, curly hair stood in front of about ten people who sat at tables forming a big rectangle. The lady began by discussing the definition of trauma and explained how we were going to later practice art therapy to unlock our thoughts and feelings regarding both positive and neg-ative moments from our past. I hadn't realized the seminar was going to be participatory but dove in without trepidation. I took notes as she was speaking.

"The definition of psychological and developmental trauma is emotional pain that cannot find a home where it can be held," she said in a quiet, assured manner. "Trauma can be, really, any negative event from one's past and doesn't necessarily have to be catastrophic or life threatening. A lot of turmoil is experienced early in our lives, and the way we feel about those things is set at an early age."

As I continued to take notes, I learned that many people bury their feelings only to find that, over time, what springs up from the ground are weeds and plants of an often-poisonous variety. You reap what you sow and in this case, buried thoughts and emotions affect the individual even though they are long out of sight and out of mind. In the case of Rachel and myself, our childhoods were rel-atively normal, but like everyone, there was some emotional pain that could not find a home.

I thought about the time I suffered a nervous breakdown in graduate school, years ago. Now, about sixteen years later, in that brown skyscraper building in downtown Chicago, I was confront-ing something again that I had tried to forget. After the woman finished her talk and we had a brief discussion, each participant received pastels and art paper. She had us reflect on a negative moment and, with our eyes closed, draw whatever came to mind, using only two of the pastel colors. I tried to draw my experience in grad school and drew a bunch of red dots and lines in between two yellow layers. I remembered the heat, the fear, and the inability to adjust. We later reflected on what we drew, and I described it as a time when I was overwhelmed by what came from within—when the emotions inside had no outlet and grew to become a force stronger than I could consciously handle. To balance out the process, we did the same thing for a positive moment and so I reflected on meeting and marrying Rachel.

"Meditation holds the mind like a mother holds an infant," the woman said as we closed our eyes. "What are you feeling inside? What are the events that led you to this place?"

I drew a green-and-purple wavy picture with some hands offering something. In the corner of the picture was a small, contained smear of red. I'm terrible at art, but luckily for this kind of therapy that didn't matter. Also fortunate for me, we were later able to open our eyes and finish our drawings. After coming up with my masterpiece, which looked as if a toddler could have created it, the lady prompted us to write a reflection.

"What am I supposed to understand by this image?" she suggested. "What is the image trying to show me? What confuses me?"

I wrote that the green represented a peaceful attitude after finally coming to a resting point in my search for love. This time in my life saw an end to the loneliness and isolation I had experienced before meeting Rachel. It also helped alleviate some of the struggles I had with establishing myself personally and professionally, and gave me a sense of maturity that I had lacked. The purple represented my wife, and the hands were the heart she offered me in order to find and feel peace. However, in the relief I felt upon settling down, I also felt frustration—relief for finally finding a soul mate, but frustration from trying to reconcile with her. I had to learn to fully accept her, form new expectations, and redefine myself. The space in the corner of my drawing represented the love and passion that was present in both of us, but perhaps hidden or buried, unable to express itself. The wavy purple lines, chaotic circles all mushed together, represented the conflict that seemed to be present within my wife and the conflict she brought to the relationship. In retrospect, the purple circular lines probably also came from within myself as well.

I left the workshop very excited to share what I had learned in the seminar with Rachel. I wanted to try this kind of art therapy technique with her to see if it could be beneficial or fun like it was for me. I was also excited to meet up with a former ESL student the next day—a pretty, quiet girl who I had no real business contacting. I had taught her English several years earlier when she had just arrived from Venezuela, and we had coffee once or twice outside of school so I could improve my Spanish.

That girl and I sat down that warm Sunday afternoon at an outside table at Bar on Buena, located in the Uptown part of Chicago—a couple blocks from the high-rise apartment building where she was staying that summer. Underneath us were two flimsy, wooden chairs. Above us, a tall, solitary tree provided a bit of shade as it arched over the sidewalk and covered part of the building's red brick exterior. We chatted about her English classes and the neighborhood; meanwhile people around us blurred together like background characters in a slowly unfolding drama. After a drink or two I convinced her that we should continue chatting back at her apartment. If I had gone to the art therapy class with a halo, I was now following this girl with horns—horns and a halo had really been the competing costumes of my wardrobe ever since I was a kid. The halo reflected societal expectations; the horns, my own desires. For some reason I felt the need to break the rules in order to get something I wanted. I was also trying to access the passion that was buried somewhere underneath those wavy, chaotic lines I had drawn in the workshop.

Inside her matchbox-sized apartment, not much chitchat was needed before I unleashed my own interests and we kissed and embraced like young lovers. Any further advances were quickly rebuffed since she knew I was married, and my protests were not convincing. Yet as I left her building less than an hour after arriving, my heart felt like it was soaring in the air. The passion that had been bottled up inside me was released, even if only for a little while, and that was enough to send me out into the world like I was floating. We didn't stay in touch, and I wouldn't hear from her again until about a year later, when the events of that day would start to unravel multiple destinies.

By the time I got home a day or so later, I acted as if nothing happened. I told Rachel how well the concert went and about meeting up with old friends of ours. I kept my remorse and guilt hidden underneath my false-yet-functional exterior. Then, out of the blue, Rachel said to me:

"Did you also meet your girlfriend?" Her mother was in town for some mother-daughter time and stood behind Rachel as she said this. Her mom laughed and said, "Oh, Rachel." It was clear that Rachel was joking, but her words were also a test to gauge my reaction. Her comment stunned me. I tried to think how she would know, or how she would even have suspected. Could she be that intuitive? I pleaded innocent and dumb, as most guys are fond of doing.

"What do you mean?" I asked her. "Why would you ask me that? There's no girlfriend," I said.

Without replying, she acquiesced and seemingly accepted my response. She didn't bring it up again, nor did I.

About a week later, I finally showed her the picture of our relationship from the art therapy class. I had largely forgotten about briefly wandering outside the bounds of marriage and instead was very proud to present to her my drawing and express my interpretations. Unfortunately, she saw it as a personal attack. The wavy purple lines were all she commented on.

"So is that what you think?" she asked. "You think I'm crazy and our relationship issues come from me?"

"No, I just feel that there's some love between us that's not coming out," I replied. "There's something preventing us from showing more love towards each other."

"Maybe if you were more affectionate and actually showed emotion, things would be better," she countered.

"Yes, but I wanted to show how you brought peace and love into my life and how I sometimes feel in the relationship."

"Well, this makes it seem like I have problems and I'm a burden. Maybe you're the one with problems," she said as she left the room to continue preparing some food in the kitchen.

During our Christmas plane trip to the West Coast several months later, we had some time to kill and a row to ourselves. I tried the same art therapy with her and after some reluctance, she finally drew a bleak looking, black picture and wrote about its significance on a separate page.

"What do you understand by the image? What is it trying to show you," I asked her.

"It's not showing me anything I don't already know. I've already analyzed my problems and I know what my issues are," she said with a hint of contempt for making her go through with this. I didn't understand why the therapy wasn't working quite like it did for me. My sense of disappointment and ineptitude grew because even though I was trying to guide her as the woman at the Institute had guided our group, something seemed lost in translation.

"Well, how do you feel after drawing and reflecting?" I asked, trying to push a little further.

"I don't feel different—just mad my life turned out this way, and sad that I didn't go about love the right way," she replied. "I don't know if I'll ever get the kind of love I'm looking for."

I recalled the time we first moved to Virginia in July of 2016. We arrived with me driving a large Penske moving truck and Rachel driving my car with Hershey and a few belongings inside. The weather was super hot and humid, and luckily the air conditioning worked inside the modern two-bedroom apartment we had secured. Our new apartment complex seemed perfect for our current living situation, but we'd had to rely on seeing a "floor model" before signing the lease because the apartment we would be moving into wasn't available yet. As a result, when we finally made the eight-hundred-mile journey from Chicago and arrived late that night with all of our belongings, Rachel had high expectations of the place. As we toured our apartment, she cried and quickly became inconsolable. The apartment was narrow with strange angles, not ideal for setting up all of our furniture. Still, Rachel's reaction was extreme. She collapsed in the corner of the living room and sobbed. I was familiar with the pain on display in front of me, as I recalled similar moments from my past—the time in grad school or when friends moved away during childhood. It was probably one of the reasons I chose un-excitement over getting my hopes up, the reason I chose non-emotion over any emotion at all. The feeling she evoked I had long buried within me. I didn't want to dredge it up. The beauty of Rachel was that she was some-one who couldn't hide her pain.

"This isn't going to work. It's not like what we saw before," she said while on her knees with tears flowing down.

"I know, but it will be fine. It's not that big a deal." I put my hand on her shoulder.

"How are we supposed to live when nothing fits?" she replied.

I couldn't make her feel better. It was as if the reality she wanted remained forever unattainable, and I wondered if there was some-thing beneath it all that played a role—something tormenting her from within. In those moments, she often called her mother because her mom was usually able to save the day. In fact, she arrived not too many days after that phone call to help us make sure the apartment, our belongings, and our life coexisted in the best way possible. She arranged the furniture perfectly, attached the TV to a wall mount, and even stayed up late that night washing dishes. Since I had to go to work the next day, Rachel spent most of the night helping her mother and admonishing her if she was making too much noise.

"Don't wake Greg up," she pleaded. "He's working tomorrow and I don't want to make him mad."

"Oh, OK. Not a problem," her mom replied.

At that moment a wasp flew into the living room from the sliding glass door, and Rachel tried to spray it before it got very far. As it flew around, the hot night became ripe with tension, since it's not easy to kill a flying wasp while being completely calm and quiet.

"Eeep!" Rachel said as she cornered it in the dining room chandelier. In the process of spraying and killing the bug, she also sprayed the dishes placed on the table underneath, which was the real reason her mom stayed up later that night washing dishes. I slept through the whole thing, only learning about all of this the next day, much to my amusement.

Throughout her life, Rachel's mother had gone above and beyond her normal mom duties to help Rachel in any conceivable way. She tirelessly assisted with schoolwork, after-school activities, and music. This included staying up all night to make costumes and outfits, staying up all night to drive for a visit, and staying up all night worrying if Rachel was going to survive her latest interpersonal drama. She showered love upon Rachel and was always there for her when she had a breakdown. One could argue there was too much involvement—it's just that with someone like Rachel, there was an overwhelming desire to protect her because she could go to such a dark, overpowering place. Rachel told me once about the abuse her mother had endured, being the only daughter in a male-dominated family of clunky, constrictive Catholics; so I think there was a common bond that each was aware of the trauma in the other—or perhaps that they both shared something that was too dark to acknowledge in words.

In a story relayed to me by her mother, a week before her high school graduation, Rachel had wanted to go live with her boyfriend, who was attending Arizona State University. Her parents said no. As her mom ironed clothes in the basement one Thursday evening, Rachel came downstairs to show what happened and explain how she didn't mean to go as far as she did.

"I wasn't trying to commit suicide; I just went too far with this," she said as she displayed a right forearm with a deep, self-inflicted gash. In that moment, both her life and her parents' lives changed forever. Even though Rachel had shown earlier signs of teenage angst, this was different. Her mother immediately grabbed a towel from the nearby bathroom and wrapped the wound tightly.

"We need to go to the hospital right now," her mother said as she felt her heart going through the floor.

No more words were spoken between them the rest of the evening. On the car ride to the hospital there were no glances exchanged, no acknowledgement of the new reality. Instead, there was dead silence. When they arrived, they were not the only family members there. Rachel's grandmother was already at the same hospital dealing with Parkinson's disease. Now Rachel, her father, her father's mother, and her own mother were all there dealing with life-and-death matters. Rachel's mom couldn't look at her. Rachel's father sat outside in the hall by himself and cried. On the one hand, there was an amazing, immensely talented young girl getting ready to go off to college. Everyone in her hometown was excited about where she would go to school and what would become of her promising musical career. On the other hand, her parents now had to consider dropping everything and putting college on hold. It was a crucial point in her life, since ultimately, the promise of her future career superseded dealing completely with the issue at hand. In the following years, her parents would invest a lot of energy and money to make sure she would make it through adulthood safely. Her new environment and the people she could rely on would determine the stability in her life. The wavy lines from the picture I would draw were covered over, issues to be dealt with over time.

A common refrain from Rachel I became familiar with years later was:

"Nobody understands. Nobody cares. Nobody wants to hear it. I could cry a thousand times and it wouldn't matter."

On one occasion after doing the dishes, she told me:

"You only love me when I do things around the house."

"Rachel, that's not true," I said.

"Yeah, you're more affectionate with me if I do the dishes or clean," she said. "My mom is the same way. She's nicer to me when I do what she wants."

She would say she didn't know why she felt so bad because she didn't do anything except be a good person. She would say she's a good person, so why was she being punished? She would say she's being kicked while she's still down because people liked to watch her suffer. The side of her that I caught a glimpse of when we started dating became more apparent because the outside world could reflect her inside world—a world of what seemed to be confusion and pain. All the insecurities buried deep inside seeped through the cracks, and her pain motivated her to create a sturdy-yet-fragile exterior. Whenever things became too much, she punished herself and made a plea with the world: "See, this is how I feel. Don't you care?"

If something upset Rachel, it seemed like there was so much emotional pain that one possible outlet for that hurt was self-harm. By the time I met her, she already had a visible mark on her leg and one on her forearm—remnants of the worst incidents, each looking as if she was bitten by a shark, but still easy to conceal. There were no more scars before we got married, but she did cut herself several more times. People who have scars from self-injury are in some ways more honest than the rest of us. At least they show to the world they have emotions and pains that are too much to handle. They allow their inner world to be seen, even if just for a moment.

Chapter 10
Marriage

*But if you tame me, then we shall need each other. To me, you
will be unique in all the world. To you, I shall be unique in
all the world.*

—Antoine de Saint-Exupéry

WHEN WE WERE in our second year of living in
Virginia, it was our third year of marriage, and even
though we still didn't have kids, at this point we were
talking about the logistics and the right time to have one. We both
had new jobs, were living in a new state, and both were trying to
navigate the perils of adulthood. Mine was teaching Spanish at a
high school forty minutes away by car. Hers, as I mentioned, was
teaching trumpet at the university and performing with the local
symphony orchestra. Part of the dilemma was that Rachel couldn't
continue to take beta-blockers for her performing job and be preg-
nant at the same time—the drug would decrease her heart rate too
much. She wasn't really able to perform without them, due to her
increased state of anxiety, both for rehearsals and performances.
Consequently, we put off the topic another year.

Instead of kids, we did what a lot of other couples do and
started with dogs. Our second dog Cookie caught Rachel's eye one
day in January of 2017, not too long after we moved to Virginia.
She was a stray who lived with a temporary family that decided to
return her when they left town. Rachel said that she knew Cookie

was a little wild based on her time with her at the shelter—she would not stop moving around and played aggressively. Whereas our dog Hershey would play and also try to cuddle when we met him the first time, Cookie just simply couldn't control herself, and excitement emanated from her wiggly little body. Rachel hoped that Hershey would get along with Cookie at a meet-and-greet, and also hoped that I would approve when I drove one day after school to see the cute new seven-month-old puppy, who had a black head, mostly-white body and a black tail with a white Q-tip ending.

Rachel had previously come to me with a pouty face and said Hershey needed a playmate. I agreed it would be nice for him to have a sister of sorts. She said that with me working long hours at school and not at home as much, Hershey was depressed. We adopted Cookie shortly thereafter, and very soon Hershey had to learn to be the sweet one while his sister replaced him as the cute one. A daily recurring scene in our bedroom after the adoption involved Cookie's new sleeping area. The medium-sized dog crate with a comfy pad for sleeping was located against the wall, just past the foot of our bed and to the left.

"Rachel, we need to put Cookie in her crate. Otherwise, it's too hard to sleep," I said one evening as I tried to deal with a puppy on top of the bed. Time after time of having a dog stuck to my leg or back in the middle of the night had worn my patience thin. Even if she started in her own spot on the bed, she inevitably would end up attached to Rachel or myself, as if she were some kind of magnet seeking a desperate connection.

"Noo," she replied with a high-pitched protest. "I feel bad putting her in the crate. She just wants to be with us." Trying to ignore her, I quickly got up, picked up a reluctant Cookie and carefully coaxed her inside the crate.

"Look at her face. She doesn't want to be in there," Rachel said as she pleaded with me to be more understanding.

"Look, I need to sleep. You need to sleep. This is best," I said.

"Can't we just leave the crate door unlocked so she doesn't feel stuck and alone?" she asked.

"No, we tried that already. She goes out and immediately comes up on the bed," I said curtly.

Cookie eventually realized her pouting looks weren't effective and went to sleep. Rachel and I would thankfully enjoy a good night's sleep as well. But as soon as Cookie woke up around 6 or 7 in the morning, she scratched at the gate and whined. She needed to be close to someone and wasn't going to take no for an answer. At that point, one of us got up and unlocked the crate door so Cookie could escape her prison of isolation. The overpowering need for contact was stronger than our ability to ignore it.

Rachel could identify with Cookie. After all, while I had picked out Hershey years ago at the shelter in Chicago, she had found Cookie and there was something in the dog that resembled Rachel's unique desire for connection at all cost. The moment I arrived home after work one day that year, I could feel Rachel studying my behavior, my tone of voice, and my body language. She gauged my mood like this most days. I walked up the stairs from our front door to the living room with a tired, blank expression on my face.

"Why didn't you put away the banana muffins last night?" she asked. She slightly opened her lips, a telltale sign that she was uncertain of something, perhaps my reaction.

"I don't know. I forgot I guess," I replied, being careful about my tone of voice. I could feel her eyes on me, trying to discern how I felt.

"I think you left them out for me to put away. I know how you are; you left them out cause you were mad I didn't come home right after rehearsal," she said.

"No, I just didn't know where to put them," I countered. I knew that I could be passive-aggressive at times, but this was not one of them. I did a double-check to see if perhaps I was mad, but I definitely wasn't. I just didn't know what to do with the banana muffins.

"Well, I can tell when you're mad and when you're being passive. Some friends and I decided to get drinks after practice," she said, being cautious to sound diplomatic and not offend.

Since she was so sure of herself, I almost believed her. Maybe she was right.

Wait a second...."But I'm not angry," I blurted out. I felt crazy, like I didn't know my own self or feelings. There was one time when I did mention something when she didn't come home right away, but that was a while ago and I wouldn't even classify that as being upset. Her eyes continued to study me. It was like I was performing on stage and didn't know my own lines.

After every phone conversation with my family, Rachel wanted to know what we talked about. It got to the point that I felt I should take notes, because she wanted to know everything. A lot of the time though, I forgot half of what my family said. At one point, she intercepted an email sent from my mother. She frequently wanted to know what my family said about her and thought that some of my mother's messages acted as a wedge between us—asserting control over me when she needed us to be on our own team.

"Impulsive! Your mom called me impulsive," Rachel said in an angry tone. "What does she really mean—that I'm emotional? Maybe she should mind her own business. She's taking your side and minimizing me."

I also didn't give Rachel much to work with. There wasn't much difference between my tone of voice when I was angry and when I wasn't. The truth was that I was just expressing my own opinion about 90's rock music she liked, and I wasn't a fan. The truth was that I did enjoy her cooking, just couldn't adequately express my thanks. The truth was that I was impressed by her musical talent, just couldn't adequately express what I felt. All of my true feelings were bottled up and what came bubbling up usually sounded mechanical—the exterior I used to defend my inner thoughts and desires was too thick.

One of the first passions Rachel shared with me was a TV series she liked. In general, we didn't have a lot of common TV shows that we enjoyed together. She watched shows like *Sex and the City*, *Say Yes To The Dress*, *Housewives of Orange County*, *The Bachelorette* and *90 Day Fiancé*. I preferred sports and documentaries. We ended up bonding over the series *Breaking Bad* and *House of Cards*, but before that, when we first started dating, Rachel tried to get me to watch her favorite TV series of all time—*Six Feet Under*. In a way, it's fitting she enjoyed that show so much, since it depicts death and dark issues in a very personal, poignant way, with the main characters working in a funeral home. We watched several episodes but I couldn't get into it, especially the more depressing it got as the main family became more dysfunctional. She was disappointed when I told her I didn't really want to watch more episodes. Her negotiations turned to pleading and when she realized my conviction, she acquiesced with a long face that understood we wouldn't be connecting on what had been one of her secret obsessions during her young adult life.

The reality was that I wanted her to be herself. For someone like Rachel though, she often conformed parts of herself to be the person she thought would win my heart. She seldom played her favorite music around me, knowing it wasn't my favorite; she eventually stopped cooking as much, seeing that it didn't create the reaction she wanted; and while she continued to perform audacious and impressive concerts, she learned to accept my reactions after her performances—the congratulatory thanks and hug, but not quite the right emotional validation or response she was looking for. Not having the right kind of mirror around meant she stopped being herself. Over time, she stopped reflecting back to me, just like I learned to stop reflecting back to the world. If life's task is simply to know and accept one's true self, you would think others would help you do just that. People unknowingly act against you to mold you into something closer to themselves, and finding someone who truly sees you is few and far between.

During our third and fourth years of marriage, Rachel was so frustrated with our communication and connection issues that she would sporadically ask me if I was autistic. She needed a reason for why I didn't show a lot of emotion or have "typical" emotional reactions. One day she showed me what "alexithymia" was (the inability to recognize or express one's emotions) and thought maybe I had that. She also wanted to know why we sometimes seemed like strangers or why we couldn't take the next step in our relationship including a house and kids.

One time, I took an online quiz she sent me, and it showed I wasn't autistic. I took the quiz to humor her, to try to get her off my back. It angered me because she was implying something was wrong with me, that I couldn't act like other people. She desperately wanted a medical explanation for why I was myself and why we weren't connecting.

On one occasion in the fall of 2017, she accused me of being autistic while we were driving home in my red Toyota Camry. We drove down Old Lynchburg Road in between the lush greenery of countless trees and bushes on either side. The vegetation was so thick you couldn't see through it, though a couple houses peaked through every so often. After a comfortable moment of silence that perhaps lasted too long, Rachel said:

"Do you think you might be autistic? Is there any family history of autism?" Her tone was clipped and direct. Although she hadn't anticipated confrontation, she soon got it.

It was a topic she had brought up one too many times and the anger quickly built up from my chest to my head. My body became warm and kindled a kind of power within that I normally don't feel—the emotions that I had buried suddenly were released. I revved up the car and accelerated really fast. I was still in control, but going well above the speed limit.

"What are you doing?" was all she could say as she gripped the door handle. Her body tensed up as I hijacked the conversation that she thought would be explorative.

I remained calm while the power of the car accelerating reverberated beneath us.

"I'm not autistic and it pisses me off when you say that," I said with clenched teeth. Something within me came to life and the diffident side of myself briefly disappeared, making way for my alter ego to surface. It appeared as if out of a fog.

"You're going to kill us," she said as we made the right-hand turn on to Sunset Avenue Extended. I quickly decelerated the car and avoided skidding. No other cars were in sight.

Both of us were silent for the remaining few minutes of the ride. I parked the car, got out, and Rachel stayed in her seat and didn't go inside. I think she needed time to collect herself and also to relay what had just happened to her mother. The experience frightened her and she didn't know what to think of me the rest of the day. I would later learn not to get angry like that. The button she liked to press wore off. When she turned from calling me autistic to calling me a psychopath, I could take it. I didn't get angry. It was the kind of insult she used to dig deeper, and I realized it was coming from a darker place.

Another day that September, we were both in our apartment after a long work week. "Hey, do you want to go to a movie?" she asked me. "I know you're probably tired from working, so we can just stay in if you want. But there's a cool documentary out and I kinda would like to see it. I understand though if you're tired."

"Oh, OK. Well, a documentary? I'm not super into seeing documentaries in the theater. Maybe though," I replied.

I spent a little bit of time with her and the dogs, decided I was too tired and that we should just stay in. I then went to go practice my trumpet for forty minutes or so. At this point it would have been easy for both of us to get sidetracked and start doing separate things—her, drinking wine and watching reality TV, me, playing my trumpet.

While playing that night, I used the practice session as an emotional release. Each note and melody that poured out of my horn was an opportunity to say what I didn't express with words. Normally if I felt sad, I played ballads. If I really felt bad, I played the blues. The sessions were so cathartic that they became crucial, not just for keeping up my musical acumen, but also my emotional health. On that particular evening, I tried to speed through

my études and scales, and skipped straight into playing interesting ideas over a blues. The angular melodies and stacked harmonic
ideas came out of my bell in a flurry. It was a cram session and I
had just enough time to emit the fire and calm fury brewing inside.
Forty-five minutes later (it was around 9:15 p.m.) I came out and
sat with her on the couch.

"Hey, what are you watching?" I asked.

"Oh, nothing. It's not important," she said before tightening
her lips. I could feel the uneasiness emanating from her—like she
had worked her brain up into tiny knots and was looking for a way
to untie them. The subject of crying came up during the episode of
90 Day Fiancé that was playing and she seized on the opportunity.

"You're too insensitive. I can't picture you crying," she said.

"It used to be easier. I don't know what's happened. I still think
I can cry a little," I replied.

"No, you're in your own world and bury your emotions," she
countered with a hint of contempt.

"Well, isn't that like your dad? Isn't he the same way—aren't
most guys like that?" I replied. It was like being an animal poked
with a stick.

"It's fine. You just don't make as much money as my dad. He
knew he needed to support his family, so he got trained in computers and ended up with a good-paying job."

"I *have* a decent paying job," I replied defensively.

"Kind of. All you do is bring work home anyway. You need a
job where you don't have to do that. You're so busy with teaching
that you don't do as much stuff around the apartment. I end up
doing most of the cleaning," she said.

Her last comment set me off. I got up from the couch.

"What do you mean, I don't do anything?" My chest tightened
and something came up from within like a wave.

"I do most of the chores. If anything gets done, it's usually me.
You put things off and then I end up doing them," she said.

"That's not true. Look, just please stop talking," I replied, as I
tried to maintain my balance.

Rachel continued to talk though. When I grabbed her by the wrist to lead her into a different room and told her she was trying to start a fight, she started hitting and kicking me. I quickly let go.

"You're such a Peter Pan," she said. "You're a privileged Christian who doesn't understand the problems of this world." She used to make these remarks when I tried to avoid talking about politics. Even though it wasn't a pleasant experience, in some respects, she was like Hades leading Persephone to the underworld; keeping me in check when I was lost in my own innocence.

After years of dating Rachel, I learned the hard way not to take the bait when she tossed me confrontational softballs. After getting tired of breaking things, I learned a new strategy and would just walk away or disengage. Sometimes walking away was what *she* did though, and in that scenario I had to become like a parent. Several weeks prior in late August, Rachel and I were at a popular bar in downtown Charlottesville, the college town where we lived. The place was usually crowded, noisy, and some kind of Americana band would be playing. As we entered, the bar on the left side of the room featured countless bottles of whiskey, stacked on a shelf against an exposed brick wall. The band was on break and the small stage in front of us only contained a few amps, a guitar, and a solitary, yet intense, looking drum set. Despite the lack of a band, it was still hard to find room to stand and talk because of the amount of people and the perturbing noise coming from inane conversations around us. We went with an unmarried couple that lived in our apartment complex and since we didn't know them that well, the evening was either going to be a bonding experience or something more mundane. It was neither.

For whatever reason, bonding in this situation took on a whole other meaning—each relationship had its faults and there was not enough stability in either one to conceal them. Everyone made decent enough small talk, but Rachel became distant. The masks each couple wore slowly came off. Eventually, the boyfriend discovered someone at the bar who had cocaine, and Rachel consumed enough alcohol to vent old relationship wounds. To be clear, nobody except the boyfriend had anything to do with drugs that night, but events quickly spiraled once vices became apparent. I don't know which happened first, the cocaine or Rachel ambushing me in public. She never had any qualms about sharing private information with relative strangers, and this was one of those times.

"My husband slept with another girl when we were dating," she blurted out.

"We had been seeing each other for just two months and were on a break," I replied in defense, feeling slightly mortified.

The girl tried to comfort Rachel and everyone else tried to figure out what just happened. I understood her pain regarding our imperfect beginning, but I always tried to justify the situation by saying it was well within the bounds of acceptable dating practice. It was an event she would bring up from time to time throughout our entire relationship. For as much as I tried to hide or disappear from her intense emotions (and mine as well), they always sought me out and confronted me, like being stopped and frisked by a belligerent police officer.

The conclusion of that night wasn't good for either couple. The boyfriend wandered off to find someone else who had drugs. Ten minutes later Rachel wandered off after drinking too much and getting upset. I tried to be as nonchalant about the whole thing as I could, but the shame was too much. While sharing vulnerabilities was Rachel's strength, it didn't always turn out well.

I excused myself to go look for Rachel. The girlfriend went to look for her boyfriend, found him in the same general area, and reined him in. I wouldn't find Rachel until hours later. I looked near the bar, but she wasn't there. I went back to the car, and she didn't go back there either. I called her on her phone and she didn't pick up. Eventually she did answer, and it seemed like she was at an intersection on foot. After that, she didn't pick up my calls. She was also practically incapacitated, so I got extremely worried. I drove around some more and called her parents. I panicked. All of the thoughts, from someone taking advantage of her to maybe being hit by a car, raced in my head and made me feel like my heart was in my throat. Her parents told me to call the police, but when I did, there wasn't anything they could do since she wasn't technically a missing person at that point.

About an hour after nervously driving around looking for her, I headed home. I found Rachel passed out on the bed. Relief washed over me—it seemed like a miracle she was there. When I went to bed that night, feelings of confusion, anger, and fear were all mixed up inside me and I didn't know what to do with them. I was mainly relieved things would be normal again the next day. In the morning she said she didn't remember how she got home, but she claimed that she walked.

"I was upset," she said—a phrase she learned to use in order to justify what had happened and avoid some of the guilt. She would also say she was tired of feeling bad for having emotions and tired of being confronted when things in the relationship seemingly didn't change. That's why I never could convince her that her actions weren't appropriate. She knew it, but she also knew how she felt and was tired of apologizing for the dilemma of dealing with her demons. If it were true that she walked home that night, it was probably a sixty-minute trek, not something she could really do after drinking that much and not something she should have been doing anyway since she was alone, at night, and a female. Somehow, she dodged a bullet.

Chapter 11
Charlottesville

The symbol is important for the unconscious mind and always has been.

—Erich Neumann, Psychologist

LIVING IN CHARLOTTESVILLE with Rachel was like living in a crater of nothingness. On the outside, the city seemed pretty, forward-thinking, and compassionate. On the inside, it didn't feel like anything. It probably didn't help that we weren't from there and had to develop new roots and new connections. Rachel, being the type of person she was, could do that. I, on the other hand, struggled a little. What made it more difficult initially was that I wasn't in Charlottesville all that much, since I worked forty minutes away in Staunton.

The journey we were on as a couple those three years was normal for most adults our age. We talked about children and also tried very hard to buy our first house. On the outside, our relationship seemed idyllic and tranquil. On the inside, it didn't feel like anything. The difficulty lay in the fact that the extreme sides of our personalities were in conflict. We never seemed to be on the same page, because both of us were too scared to confront our own fears and insecurities—at least, we never confronted them without self-destructing first. Why was it so difficult for me to express emotions and say, "I love you"? Why was it so difficult for her to avoid extreme reactions and outbursts? We each could be ourselves around each other and enjoy each other's company, but could never really get to the core of our own issues and identities. I suppose nobody really wants to confront parts of their unknown face and that is the reason why some are forced to do it while kicking and screaming.

In August of 2017, five days before our three-year anniversary, Rachel was going to go for a run downtown and for some reason decided against it. We still didn't know what was going on until later that Saturday morning. I randomly turned on the TV and it was all over the news—a white-supremacy rally had turned violent when protesters and counter-protesters confronted each other in a downtown area near an old Confederate statue of Robert E. Lee. As we watched, we were both shocked and in disbelief. A friend of mine from Chicago texted me and asked what the hell was going on. He also implored me to go downtown and protest, but I replied this might not be the best protest to join in.

I later took a break and escorted the dogs to the dog park located in our apartment complex. The space was big, as far as dog parks go, situated underneath a giant power line. While I was at the fenced-in patch of grass and bark located just down the hill from our place, a bunch of news helicopters flew over the downtown area. The apartment complex sat on one of the many hills of Charlottesville, and it was possible to see at least some parts of the city from where we were located. A couple of police helicopters flew close to the news choppers and closely monitored the chaos below. My attention shifted to what the dogs were doing and when I looked up again, one of the police helicopters spiraled like a paper airplane. It was out of control and spiraling down very fast. What was happening in front of me didn't register—it was such a strange spectacle for a Saturday morning. The next thing I knew the helicopter disappeared out of sight. A few seconds later, I understood, because there was smoke coming up from the ground. The day was turning into a tragedy. People popped out of their apartments one by one to see what was going on. C'ville was somehow like a war zone.

The Charlottesville riot forced the city to take a hard look at itself. Where was the hatred coming from? Why? How should they move past it? Many contentious city council meetings followed. People were angry and wanted someone to blame. Eventually, the chief of police resigned. Over time, the city learned how to better contain such protests and how to prevent further ones from taking place. Just as Rachel and I learned how to cope with our issues—but not solve them—through marriage therapy, the city also set up boundaries without a true remedy.

If you visited the park where it all took place, even a couple years after the riot, you could still see the statue of Lee, the epicenter of the clash. The city tried to cover it with a plastic tarp, but that proved unsuccessful, since it is much easier to mask one's true self than a giant, twenty-foot statue. Later, the city simply roped off the area, and it looked like it was under construction. The actual process of removing the statue got caught up in a legal battle where lawyers and judges of differing opinions were assigned the responsibility of its fate. Did the statue reflect racism and hatred, or was it just a statue? Was it just a statue, or did it represent the mythological aspirations of a defeated South? The community was dealing with its own unknown face.

I wondered why such a tragedy occurred that August in Charlottesville. It seemed like there was something going on underneath that had pulled things down and caused them to spiral. There was the police helicopter—there was our relationship. What could do such a thing, and was it related to something hidden or underneath?

The coexisting drama within our relationship also came to a head that summer. That's what the dilemma was about later the following spring—that's why we went to marriage therapy. In her frustration she conveyed a message of regret; and in a note she wrote during the art therapy technique I tried with her, she said:

I chose to get married to someone I didn't have the kind of connection with I desired because I thought no one else would love me. Now I trust in my self and see my worth and believe I could find that kind of connection with someone else. I feel sad that I went through this and to have an effect on another person's life. I still don't know what the right thing to do is— stay with someone who was there for me without a connection, or move on and find the connection I had been searching for before I got diagnosed.

She initially tried to keep me from seeing what she wrote, and when I eventually did read it, my reaction was disbelief. I don't think it completely registered, what she was saying. She told me several weeks later in a drunken state that she only got married to me because of the STD. We had gone to Washington D.C. to watch a baseball game between the Nationals and visiting Cubs, and after the game had found a small bar nearby to prolong the evening and spend time. It was supposed to be a fun trip to see my favorite team, but as she sat across from me while we were seated at the small table near the entrance, she proceeded to explain that she probably wouldn't have married me if she had been in a better place, both physically and emotionally.

My reaction was silence and casual acceptance, since she had only expressed something that had been in the back of both of our minds for quite some time. I also knew that in these situations, it was best not to make a scene or provoke her more, since I was really not equipped to defend myself and had not previously prepared anything in the event something like this would happen. The next morning was spent nursing my wounds and waiting a long time to use the restroom at our Airbnb (the owner had doubled up the reservation and allowed the next tenant to arrive while we were still there). After leaving the rented apartment and having an awkward exchange with the newly-arrived bathroom squatters, we went to the train station to return to Virginia. When Rachel went to buy coffee or juice, I wandered around aimlessly, trying to keep my distance from her—trying to express anger and at the same time hide that inside I was depressed. It was like my world had caved in on me and there was no light coming through. I didn't speak to her at all that morning and just couldn't comprehend that our relationship had gotten to that point. The train ride home was mostly silent—it resembled all of those other moments when she would vent her true feelings; I would be left wounded, and then we would slowly have to repair the distance that now existed between us. When I asked her a week or so later if what she said was correct, she said that it wasn't entirely true and that there was more to it than that—all things that would have been better expressed in the moment.

We were at a cliff that summer—a point in the relationship where, as high as we had climbed, we were still somehow on a dangerous ledge looking down at the chasm beneath. Both of our worst nightmares had come true. Hers was not being in a passionate relationship that had lots of connection, while mine was being in a relationship where my partner slowly rejected me as a person. The extreme ways our personalities dealt with conflict pushed us away from each other, further away from the common bond that we still shared.

Chapter 12
The Email

Consciousness is like a snowball sitting on an iceberg.
—Timothy Wilson, Professor of
Psychology, University of Virginia

By June 2018, about a year after the illicit encounter with the girl from Venezuela, Rachel and I had been in marriage therapy for a couple months. The sessions were working, and allowing us to see some of our communication issues and how to improve upon them. However, one of the other reasons we were in therapy was to get me out of my shell and figure out how we could connect on a deeper level. The question the therapist put to me was, "What did I want out of life?" That was my homework, so to speak. I had to figure out what I wanted and listen to the feelings I'd learned to bury.

One question I asked myself internally, among others, was why did I seek something outside of the marriage—why did my heart lead me in that direction? While I never had sex with anyone else during our marriage, I sometimes acted like I was single, and wasn't completely loyal. I had also had a short affair during our first or second year of dating that Rachel never knew about, even though I think she intuited it. It would seem that I didn't love her enough, but I felt that I did—there just seemed like something was missing. As Lorca said in his play: *"We're all curious about what might hurt us."*

During my pondering, I had a childhood flashback to a moment with my junior high school baseball team. The field we played on was just behind the school—an expansively large field with adjacent soccer and football fields. Looking over the uneven, green baseball diamond was Thompson Hill—a large, yellow, dry hill of sagebrush and tumbleweed. The only thing on the hilltop was a large, lonely house that oversaw the action below, like a giant overseer monitoring the plebeians. The climate was arid, windy, and sunny most days—ideal for baseball and being outside. But day after day of going to baseball practice after school and listening to our coach bark out orders began to wear on some of us. Some of us talked of skipping practice one Friday. We thought we could explain our absence later without getting into trouble.

The thing we wanted to do instead was play street hockey in our friend's driveway, with little hockey sticks and a puck made from a duct-taped container of bubble tape. During this game, we didn't have to follow many rules, listen to a baseball coach, or do drills. Instead, we got to play and have as much fun as we could muster. So, one Friday, we skipped. It was myself and two other friends who were on the baseball team. Two others met us in the driveway to play, since they weren't on the team.

I felt elated—happy to not be at practice and glad to be playing. The tension and excitement forced me into a state of giddiness, and as we left school that day and walked home, my heart raced until we passed the baseball field. When we got to the fruit orchards well-clear of the field, I was able to breathe clearly, and energy bubbled up inside. Our friend lived in a unique neighborhood house that looked like it used to be a Pizza Hut—the unnatural oblong roof covered a seemingly normal-looking rectangular house. When we started to play in my friend's driveway, we ran in tight little circles, trying to evade defenders and shoot the puck. We wacked and double-wacked our sticks until the game really got going. But a friend of mine, the one whose driveway we were playing in, hit my chin with his stick and sliced it open at the bottom. I kept playing even though it stung a lot. I dabbed the cut with my shirt and tried to prevent more blood from coming out. Slowly though, my friends convinced me to stop the game and go inside to tend to the wound. Reality set in.

I needed to go to the hospital and eventually get stitches. Now, the prospect of being able to explain playing hooky from baseball practice was impossible. There was the explanation to my mother who took me to get stitches. The next day we had practice, I also had to explain to the coach about the bandage on my chin and how we decided to skip and how we were sorry about the whole thing. I tried to be mischievous but life seemingly put me in my place.

"Straighten up and fly right," life seemed to be telling me. "Otherwise, you'll get wacked on your chin and have to get stitches." Surely, one didn't cause the other. But it seemed like it did.

Now older, I was dealing with a similar dilemma. I had ventured outside the straight path and deviated from what I knew was the right thing to do. Would I be punished again for my actions— what would life's response be now? Why did I go off the road again when the markers were so clearly evident, and the consequences always so imminent? Was something at the core of me trying to break through—was something inside trying to stay alive?

I wasn't able to come up with an adequate response to my internal question, because my main theory was that I was just trying to have my cake and eat it too. What I understood at the time was that I was finally ready to let go of selfish desires and move on to have a better future with Rachel. This is what I told her, but my answer was not full of conviction. Then, while I was doing the therapy homework that first day of June, she intercepted an email.

"Greg, who's this from?" she asked me as she looked at the email on my computer. I had given it to her to look at the electronic copy of our new apartment lease extension, which was only emailed to me.

"Oh, just one of my former students—someone I used to teach a while ago in Chicago."

"Well, what is the message saying?" she asked—the email was in Spanish.

"Just 'What's up? How's things going?' Nothing more than that," I replied.

"Well, why are you emailing her in the first place?"

"She's someone that helped me with my Spanish, and I keep in touch about once a year."

"I thought you stopped meeting with girls in cafés."

"We never met in a café. This was at the school," I replied, trying to lie my way out of the mess I was now in.

I don't know if I subconsciously wanted her to see the email, but I thought nothing would come of it since it was an email to a girl I knew—just a friendly "what's up" and nothing more. But it was also the girl I had pushed boundaries with, and I had been trying to figure out the riddle of my own heart, seeing how I felt by contacting her. At that point, my mistake became evident. My heart had led me in the wrong direction, and I eventually said to Rachel that I wanted to have a future with her. Why would I even think of pursuing a Venezuelan girl who was now living in Chile, when I had built a life with someone I considered to be my best friend and soulmate? However, what to me was an innocent email, to Rachel was a smoking gun. She had again seen something underneath—the side of me who could be a selfish jerk. She was probably perplexed at how I also could be so different than the person she thought she knew. She soon chipped away and discovered the truth about what had been happening. That was why she was on my computer anytime I was away from the apartment that summer. I struggled to keep her from the whole truth because I didn't know what it would do to her or how she would react—obviously, I was also trying to protect myself and keep my own head above water. We were slowly heading to a point of no return because, as spring turned to summer and our marriage therapy sessions got more intense, the snowball that was my conscious life seemed like it was slowly melting and getting swallowed up by the iceberg underneath.

Chapter 13
The Slow Decline

"How poor indeed is man," thought he in his heart, "how ugly, how wheezy, how full of hidden shame!"
—Zarathustra in Freidrich Nietzsche's *Ugliest Man*

ONE MORNING THAT June, after Rachel had discovered the email and started her search for the truth, the dogs and I went on a run. It had rained the previous day but was just dry enough to go on one of the nearby trails. One of the places I enjoyed going running with my dogs was an old, overgrown park called Penn Park. It had an exercise trail down the hill from a picnic area and then, if you continued past the exercise trail, there was a loop trail that doubled back through the nearby golf course. Cookie, Hershey, and I walked through the exercise trail, over a creek and up a short hill. The abundance of trees and vegetation made the whole area like a jungle, and the trail weaved through the wild and untamed Virginia forest with a sense of desperation. It was a path we had taken many times before, so this day should have been no different than all the others.

Cookie, of course, was in front, always wanting to be the leader; I was in the middle, and Hershey went at his own pace in the rear. The dogs were extensions of me, connected by medium-sized leashes as I ran haphazardly with them down the first hill leading to the creek bed. Cookie pulled with all the exuberance of a hyper young dog, and Hershey made sure we didn't get too far ahead of ourselves. Not long after we passed the creek on our left, my foot hit a rut in the ground, and I tripped going full speed, flailing hands-first into the ground. I sat there for a moment in stunned silence as I tried to figure out what had happened. My scraped hands and arm, and my bruised right knee stared back at me with vengeance. The dogs had also stopped in their tracks and looked at me as if they were wondering when I was going to get back up. It reminded me of what was going on in my life at the time. I was going along minding my own business, but all of a sudden—I was flat on my face. What had happened a year ago and prior to that was catching up to me. I wondered, even, if I had somehow tripped myself and why I would do that.

A week or so later, Rachel sat at the glass dining-room table one evening with her computer in front of her. Her schedule that academic year was grueling. She performed a recital and a concerto with the orchestra, had numerous other performances with said orchestra, fulfilled her duties as music librarian, taught private trumpet lessons, coached a small brass ensemble, and of course did side gigs to supplement our income. The finale of her season of obligations was a Pops concert, which took place every year at the beginning of June. She was ready to be done. She was exhausted and couldn't fathom taking on any more commitments.

Her face was stoic, and I could tell she was masking her inner turmoil. The lights above the glass table were bright and highlighted her angry features. I was confused. Normally she would be happy about finally finishing her last work obligation.

"So, how's it going?" I asked, trying to gauge her mood.

"Fine," she replied, looking straight ahead at the computer.

"What are you up to?" I asked.

"Just replying to some emails and figuring things out," she said. There was a brief pause, followed by: "How long did you know that girl from the email?"

"Rachel, I don't know, maybe a couple years."

"Did you go out with her before?"

"No, look, it's not that important. I wanted to see if you felt like celebrating—getting a drink or something."

"I don't know if that's a good idea. I'm not in a good mood," she said.

"Come on. It'll make you feel better. I know how hard the year has been, and we should celebrate," I replied as I stood across the table facing her.

"OK. But only if we promise not to talk about anything negative—nothing about our problems. If I start to do that, please remind me," she said.

I agreed whole-heartedly to that condition, and we went to a nearby bar, called Timberwood Tap House, to celebrate the end of her busy year. The establishment was a trendy place only about a year old. It featured drop-down LED lights that looked like little microphones. Behind the bar there was exposed brick, but also wood paneling and several TV screens that intruded on the conversation if you let them. We both ordered a whisky on the rocks, which was a drink fitting for the occasion but not for the person. We were having a good time and really enjoying each other's company for the first time in a while. In a way, it was like we were dating again. The smell of the whisky was strong, yet comforting.

Not long after Rachel started her second whisky, she changed. Her eyes became distant and a little glossy—her body more alert and on edge. It was almost like another side of her took over and didn't let up. She asked me about the other girl from the email.

"Who is this girl? Did you have sex with her? What does she look like?"

I glanced to my left at the bartender in front of the exposed brick, and tried to gauge if he could hear our conversation. I reminded her we weren't going to talk about that.

"Why did you contact her? What did she say to you?" she continued.

Once again, I told her we weren't going to talk about that. She didn't relent, however, and became angry. When I didn't adequately respond to her questions, she gave me a dirty look and pushed me.

I stood up as my natural defensive reaction but also to make sure I
didn't fall off the barstool. It was a mistake coming to the bar and
my objective quickly changed to paying the bill and getting out of
there. The storm that was coming wasn't going to be pretty.

By the time we got to the front door (which was an accomplish-
ment), Rachel was hitting me with random swipes that connected
sporadically. The surging rage within not only took over herself and
our evening, but also the overly lit, stale atmosphere of the bar. The
bartender and several other customers quickly took notice, and the
background entertainment, which had been coming from the TV,
suddenly switched to what was going on between Rachel and I.
After we got in the car, I couldn't get the car started because she
was using the advantage of proximity to make direct contact with
some of her punches. Some of the wait staff at the bar and a few
patrons came out to watch the spectacle. Rachel landed one of her
punches near my right eye and I deflected the rest with my right
arm—I ended up with a black eye for a good week or two. While I
drove off with my left hand and evaded the gaze of the onlooking
bystanders in the background, I felt the shame and ridicule that
she probably wanted me to feel. If this was the punishment for my
actions, then so be it.

However, the punishment wasn't over. When we got home,
she told me I had nullified all seven years of our relationship by
continuing to meet with girls in cafés. She proceeded to take our
wedding photo album and burn it in the fireplace. I wanted to stop
her, but even if I had tried, she would have destroyed it somehow.
It took her maybe fifteen or twenty minutes to burn the album.
In the end, there were just a few pieces that hadn't burned and a
few recognizable photos, all crumpled and distorted. I didn't know
how much more punishment she had for me, but it was enough.
Feelings of remorse settled at the bottom of my soul. I felt defeated
as I sat on the couch with my elbows on my knees, watching the
flames and Rachel's infuriated face.

Not many nights after that episode, Rachel and I were arguing
while she was in the kitchen and I was in the dining room. This

time she wasn't as heated or charged up as before. The place she occupied was a tiny, interior space where one could look out past the small kitchen bar area to the other side of the dining room where I stood. The only object I could see next to her from my vantage point was a cracked blender, repaired with glue. At some point during our argument she took off the glasses she occasionally wore, and once again, her face seemed distant. Her eyes had a wild quality, like a trapped animal. Not long after the argument started, she began to cry silent tears. She then reached over and grabbed a knife from the knife rack.

"Rachel," I said, my throat getting tighter. "What are you doing?" My voice was soft, trying not to provoke her.

"You don't care," she said between sobs.

"That's not true," I responded. I slowly got closer to her, watching her every movement. Luckily, I was close enough. She turned her back to the sink as if to brace herself and lifted her arm with the knife. As her arm came down to plunge the knife into her stomach, I lunged and reached for her arm to prevent the knife from going in too deep. While I couldn't grab her arm completely, I was able to hold it enough to deflect some of her intention. The kitchen knife punctured her abdomen on the right side of her body though, and we immediately had to address the wound.

The injury brought Rachel back to her senses and the tension that was built up inside her seemingly leaked out of the self-inflicted puncture. We went to the bathroom and as she carefully lowered the top part of her pants, I looked for gauze and other bandage supplies.

"Is it bleeding?" I asked. "How deep is it?"

"No, it's not bleeding much. But I can't really tell how deep," she said. Her voice sounded like she was far away, as if she was observing herself from a distance. She was calm, but disappointed.

"Do we need to go to the hospital?" she asked me. "It's not bleeding really. I don't really want to go to a clinic or anything like that."

"I don't know, is there any internal injury?" I asked. "How do you feel?"

"It seems fine, just hurts a little," she replied.

I found the needed supplies below the bathroom sink, and she bandaged the wound like her nurse training had taught her. We decided to be careful to make sure it didn't get worse, and then went to bed to sleep off the hysteria of the night. After Rachel fell asleep, I lay there in disbelief with thoughts racing through my head. How did that happen? What are we supposed to do now? Do I tell someone? The following morning, there was a small blood-stain on the bedsheet from when the bandage had shifted during the night. Rachel would be her normal self when she woke up. She always was.

She frequently tried to play off these episodes like nothing had happened. It was almost like there was a separation between the two sides of herself. This time was different, and we talked about her self-destruction.

"What do you think I should do?" she asked me with a nervous, defeated tone.

"I don't know. Did it get worse or is it still the same?" I asked.

"There's just some bruising. I don't really want to go to a hospital because then I'll have to tell them how it happened."

We eventually decided it wasn't necessary to go to the hospital or a clinic, but that we should monitor the wound to make sure it wasn't more serious than we thought. I told her later:

"Rachel, look. There's something inside you that's trying to kill you—and that's not normal."

I stood facing her, across from where she was sitting on the bed. She gave me a blank stare, seemingly not registering the seriousness of the situation.

"What can you do to keep this from happening again?" I asked her.

At that point she mentioned she wasn't going to drink. That was her usual response in the aftermath of these crises. While she also did a lot of yoga and other self-care techniques, drinking provided too much of a release from the stress and pain of everyday life. It always lured her back.

I immediately recalled one night earlier that winter, when I had tried to confront her about her actions under the influence. I got fed up with how much alcohol would change her behavior, so I took a bottle of vodka from the freezer and went to the balcony that overlooked the grassy patch of backyard and small forest beyond that. I threw the bottle as hard as I could into the woods. The bottle disappeared into the pitch-black night and when I later tried to find it amongst the trees and brush, it had already disappeared, like a token offering in a deep, dark well.

"Look, the drinking has to stop," I said that night after she realized the bottle of vodka was gone.

"The way I feel doesn't change regardless of whether I'm drinking," she replied in an angrily defensive manner. "That's how I feel all the time! You can't tell me what to do."

Needless to say, she didn't want to be parented. Consequently, she started to hide the alcohol. There was wine hidden in her closet. I found beer cans amongst trumpet mutes. Eventually I gave up. My efforts were futile and the situation would have to be managed another way.

At the end of February, I got a call late one Thursday night from the police that woke me up.

"Mr. Duncan I just wanted to inform you that your wife had a car accident this evening and is OK, she is fine. There were no others involved. She's currently in a holding cell though, waiting to sober up. Not sure if she'll be able to be released tonight but I can give you a phone number and they can give you more information."

"Wait, what?" I said in a confused tone. "What happened? Is she OK?" I asked.

"Yes, she is fine. Not sure what happened exactly, but some people noticed that she drove her car in a ditch and called the police. When they arrived, she was very distressed. They tried to help her but she did not pass any of the sobriety tests—car is in the process of being towed."

Apparently that night she had met up with colleagues after rehearsal, and probably drank on an empty stomach or drank one more than normal. I called several numbers before getting the right person at the police station. They informed me she could not be released until the morning since her blood alcohol level was still too high. It was agonizing, thinking about her sobering up in jail and not being able to be there for her. Just like a lot of negative events in her life, I didn't know what it would do to her or how she would respond. I lay awake thinking about her crying by herself in a jail cell, and didn't really sleep that night. I remembered the previous time she went to the hospital for over-drinking when we were dating, and wondered why again.

As morning came, I knew she needed me, but I also had to work and didn't feel I could take the day off. Maybe this would be the end of her drinking and she had learned the hard way. A trusted colleague picked her up and when I finally saw her, I tried to negotiate giving her comfort and sympathy while having some tough conversations. I couldn't gauge the shame and hurt the accident caused her. I wondered if the DUI damaged her more than the car because she didn't really want to talk about what happened and later became worried they would find out at the university.

After these incidents when she pushed herself to the edge, she stopped drinking for a while and never drove if she had even just one. I think the void she felt was too much because eventually she needed a release. She slowly returned to drinking more than she should. It started with a drink after the music festival she coordinated in March. She allowed herself one since she was celebrating with colleagues. A month or two later, that one turned into two. Later in the summer, two turned into whatever she needed to deal with the pain.

Rachel's knife accident in June and everything else that happened was traumatic. But it really wasn't that atypical of her to have extreme reactions, and I thought she could get away from harming herself as long as we didn't get into arguments and I was careful with her. We desperately needed a vacation.

Chapter 14
Summer in Montana

Through scientific understanding, our world has become dehumanized. Man feels himself isolated in the cosmos…His immediate communication with nature is gone forever, and the emotional energy it generated has sunk into the unconscious.
—Carl Jung

BESIDES THE GIRL from the email, one of the other conversations Rachel and I had that June in 2018 was about where to spend our summer vacation. We still hadn't made plans yet because we were both busy up until the end of May and beginning of June. For me, going on vacation meant going somewhere where you could take your mind off your troubles and have some new adventures. For Rachel, going on vacation meant the stress of traveling and the stress of spending time with someone you don't necessarily flow with. The one positive thing was that she got to spend time with me when I was more myself and not in "work-mode," as she called it.

In the end, I was able to arrange for Rachel to go to her cousin's wedding in Wyoming. After the wedding, I met up with her in nearby Montana for a trip to Glacier National Park. I booked a cruise to Alaska for us later on in July. The trip to Italy that she was interested in seemed like it would be too complicated and too costly. For some reason, I thought the scenery in Montana and Alaska would be a good remedy for our relationship problems. For all the amazing scenery Montana provided, Alaska was that times two. While she was initially upset about not going to Italy, she eventually conceded.

At that point, Rachel was still uncovering the details of my past indiscretions, and I was trying to downplay everything. She knew that I had kissed another girl but did not know about me meeting anyone else prior to that. By the time we arrived in Montana, it was almost like a normal vacation, and the majestic scenery did indeed provide a little bit of a distraction from our complicated problems. Rachel's plane got rerouted up to Seattle and she later backtracked, so we arrived in Missoula at slightly different times that sunny day late in June. I had already arrived several hours earlier and killed time at a local restaurant by a river, which had several kayakers trying to kayak in place against the raging rapids that eventually pushed them downstream. The sun bounced off their helmets and the water looked like a liquid conveyor belt. Each kayaker took their turns dropping in and seeing how long they could last before they eventually were no match for the strength of the unrelenting flow.

She came down the exit ramp at the airport and looked tired from her delay. She immediately searched my face for a hint of excitement and emotion, anything she could latch on to as a sign of hope. My face was blank though, despite being happy to see her. Any emotion I felt inside was blocked by an ingrained process of checks and balances—I had learned all too well how to get by with giving little. We then drove up to Whitefish and talked about the upcoming trip and other mundane stuff that acted like filler, since our chemistry was a little off. Only a week prior, I had signed us up for one of those group excursions on the Middle Fork Flathead River that traversed Glacier National Park. A day after arriving in Whitefish, we showed up at the rafting company's office about thirty minutes early. There were a mixture of tourists and tour guides in front of the small building, which resembled a cabin—some were sitting on nearby picnic benches while they tried on helmets and tried to figure out what to do with personal belongings.

"Can you hold my phone while I put on some lotion?" Rachel asked me.

"Sure," I replied. I had already put a little sunblock on my face, but being a redhead meant that Rachel always took longer trying to protect herself from the sun's harsh rays.

"Can you rub some on the back of my neck?" she said. She wore a purple t-shirt along with some workout pants and tennis shoes.

"Yeah," I replied. "Do you think we should sit in front?"

"Oh, I don't know. It depends. What are the rapids like?"

"They're not bad. Mostly class two, maybe a little class three."

"Are those wetsuits available?" she asked me. The weather was sunny but still cool. The water of course would be ice cold.

"I don't know. Maybe we should ask."

One of the tour guides announced that the 1 p.m. group should assemble by the bus. "Excuse me, do you think we'll need a wetsuit?" I asked the lanky, college-aged guide.

"Nah, you won't need them," he said. "Not unless you plan on going in the water. I mean, you can. Some people float alongside the raft but usually just for a little bit."

As we left on the buses to travel to the put-in point, we could see a larger group of tourists getting ready for their tour, scheduled right after our own. Many of them were putting on wetsuits that another guide handed out.

When we finally got the raft in the water, there were about seven of us or so, not including the guide. The raft guide was an older man retired from the military, and he had been working the rivers for awhile. He was still in decent shape, with a patch of gray, frizzled hair on each side of his balding head. Even though he had a salt-and-pepper mustache, thus giving him a more distinguished look, his face didn't express a lot of emotion when he spoke and one could argue it was a blank canvas. It was his voice that commanded respect.

"OK, let's practice some commands before we shove off," he said in a gravelly voice. "If I say 'high-side right' I want you to lean with your body to the right side—make sure to still keep your feet nice and grounded below. Remember, there's a space on the bottom of the raft where you can tuck your feet in. If I say 'high-side left', lean with your body to the left side. You don't have to physically move to either side, but make sure you're putting all your weight into it." There were a few minutes of practice and when we announced where we were all from, the guide continued.

"All right, when I say 'high-five' I don't want you to turn to the person next to you and give them a high-five with your hand. Why do you think that is?" he asked one of the kids seated next to him.

The kid smiled and looked nervously at his parents.

"Are we on land or in a boat?" the guide continued.

"A boat," the kid said.

"That's right! And in a boat we don't high-five with our hands. We high-five with our oars. So everybody, when I say 'high-five' we're going to all put our paddles up high in the middle and give everyone a high-five."

"High-five!" he shouted. Rachel and I smiled and put our oars high up in the middle of the raft and clapped the other paddles around us. It was a cute bonding exercise and while the ordeal embarrassed me, Rachel thoroughly enjoyed it.

As we took off on our journey, we realized that it was going to be mostly an easy float, with perhaps three or four places where the rapids were more difficult. The river cut through a small canyon with jagged rocks on either side of us. Above the rocks sat green pine trees ascending upwards toward hills and small mountains. Since it was a relatively narrow river, the water rushed forward with good speed, and there were many places where the whitewater carried our raft with a benign purpose. We were enfolded by nature on all sides, and floating down the river that day in late June felt peaceful and also like being immersed in a channel with no end. We were now in God's hands, and our only connection back to the real world was our trusty old guide.

"Are there any dangerous parts of the rapids?" I asked him.

"You know, I've been floating these waters for over ten years," he said. "You guys are safe as long as you do what I say." Not much later, he offered a preface to instructions for the upcoming chute.

"I remember years ago, another guy I know—experienced rafter too—ended up tipping over at this spot. The water was higher back then and he couldn't handle the flow. Well, there's a tricky spot once you go past this rock, and if you don't hit it right, it'll start to flip the raft over."

This got my attention. I think his story put everyone else on alert too, because the atmosphere in our raft became a little more anxious. Rachel had goose bumps on her arm and sat stiffly in front of me with oar in hand. If he didn't say another word about dangerous parts of the river or past accidents, people would have forgotten and the anxiety would have gone away. But the old guide continued to drop subtle reminders about the dangers ahead. Perhaps that was his way of keeping everyone on their toes, though it definitely made the mood more tense and less enjoyable.

We approached the chute he was talking about, and there was a rock sticking out into the river on our right side. The wild water now pushed us forward with unrelenting speed and as the raft slowly started to careen towards the rock, our guide barked out instructions.

"Dig in!" he shouted at us. "Harder."

Everyone paddled harder, but we hit the rock. The next thing I knew, we were heading through the chute backwards, without being able to see where we were going. I continued to paddle hard, but at this point the boat was subject to the torrent underneath and I could no longer do anything but hold on. The raft tilted to one side slightly, though not enough to tip over. If anyone was in real danger, it would have been from their own fear and anxiety.

As we slid through and floated downstream twenty yards, everyone took a sigh of relief and smiles reappeared on our faces.

"That was fun," the kid said. Some people laughed. We continued in a much similar fashion for the rest of the journey but about three-quarters of the way, the guide asked Rachel a question.

"Hey, are you cold? I can see you don't look too comfortable."

"Oh, just a little," she said with a tiny embarrassed laugh. "I'm fine."

"Are you sure? I have some extra t-shirts in this bag. Why don't I toss you one so you're not so cold?"

"OK. That would be great actually," Rachel said. She added another layer and put on the shirt and immediately felt better. I had known she was cold but hadn't realized how uncomfortable she was because I was too focused on my own anxiety. When we got to our extraction point, it was a little warmer and the sun no longer competed with high mountaintops to reach us.

"Man, it would have been nice if that guy back at the office had given me a wetsuit when we asked about it," Rachel said.

"Yeah, I guess he didn't know how cold it was," I said. "I was also pretty cold, but only for a little bit. I was more on edge than cold. Did you listen to all the stories that guide told us?"

"Yeah, he didn't help things."

On that day in June, Rachel and I made it through the rapids of the Middle Fork Flathead River. She was cold and trembling with goose-bumps for a good part of the trip, while I was trying to calm my nerves after thinking about worst-case scenarios brought up by our guide. Rachel was probably too proud to ask for help and to tell anyone that she was the most uncomfortable one in the boat. After all, she was a team player and also had a tough-it-out mindset. On the other hand, I was not in control of myself enough to relax and enjoy the trip. I also was too focused on my own uneasiness to see that Rachel wasn't protected enough from the cold and all of nature's harsher elements. In our marriage it was much the same way. The only difference was that Rachel got to the point where she was looking for help and looking for answers. She needed a way to get out of that river and into the warmth.

Our stay in Whitefish reminded us both of our honeymoon in Lake Tahoe. Both places were known for their ski resorts, and in the summertime they offered similar activities against the backdrop of never-ending green pine trees and steep mountainous terrain.

In Whitefish, in addition to our whitewater rafting adventure, we ventured to an outdoor ropes course, aptly named an aerial adventure park. The smell of pine and red cedar trees made your nose prick up, and the dry air seemed to suck the ambient noise out of the background. After putting on safety harnesses and learning the basics, we were up in the trees—sometimes ziplining from suspended platform to platform, sometimes traversing intricate bridges made of rope and wire. We had a great time at the beginning. As we kept going through the course, things got more difficult. This course was a little different than the one we had tried on our honeymoon.

"Oh God," Rachel said as she clung to a trapeze bar that transported her through the trees with her feet dangling below.

"Just hold on," I said, after making the first journey over. "It takes you straight here."

She glided over with apprehension on her face. "Oh God," she said again as she reached the platform. Since we were getting tired and had already been there for an hour or so, we were about ready to leave. However, there was another part of the course we hadn't tried. I was up to the challenge even though I knew it would be difficult. It was a single long wire going about fifty yards from one platform to the next. The only thing to hold on to was a wire trellis suspended above. If you leaned on the trellis too much, you needed a lot of balance and upper body strength to keep yourself up.

When we climbed up a narrow ladder to get to the other platform, she asked me: "Why do you want to try this again?"

"I just want to see if we can do it."

As I walked out onto the wire my confidence wavered, since the task at hand seemed more difficult than anticipated. The metallic line initially felt sturdy beneath my feet, but once I got going the stiff cord proved wobbly if not stepped on the right way. Halfway through I was exhausted, and I lost my balance. My body lunged forward and as the wire underneath wobbled, I grasped harder on the trellis above. All of a sudden, the prospect of falling gave me a sense of panic, and my desperation forced me to try harder. Even though I had a harness I didn't really feel like falling off of a wire and trying to get back up after hanging below. Falling would have made it more difficult to get to the end. If I looked back or looked down, the task of crossing became next to impossible, and if I had learned anything about life up to that point, it was that looking forward and ahead was the only way to make it. The only way to keep going was to not look back—you try to outrun your regrets and demons and just hope that they don't catch up to you when you make it to the other side.

Once my balance and composure returned, I started to focus on shuffling one foot over at a time while moving horizontally across the wire. Keeping my eyes focused on the end platform, a steady rhythm took over and helped me make it to the other side.

"I didn't think I was going to make it," I shouted to Rachel on the other side.

"I don't know if I should try," she said. At least she had the advantage of watching me navigate the circus act and she could learn from my mistakes.

"You have to slide your feet over slowly one at a time," I said. I continued to give her instructions and encouragement. She had a few small missteps, but her journey over the metallic cord went a little more smoothly than mine. She seemed tired and thankful that she got through it without falling.

"That was hard," she said. "I wobbled a little bit too much a couple of times and my arms are exhausted."

There was a moment suspended in midair on that wire that I didn't think we would both make it over, but we did. It required a lot of determination, strength, patience, and courage. Somehow we walked that tight rope and made it through that day. Similar to the rafting trip, the gauntlet we had just run piqued my anxiety and both of us were worn out. Maybe it was too much—maybe I pushed us too far, so we left to go find a bar and have a happy hour beverage.

Chapter 15

Summer in Virginia

The plants, rocks, fire, water, all are alive. They watch us and see our needs. They see when we have nothing to protect us and it is then that they reveal themselves and speak to us.
                                                    —Apache storyteller

WHEN WE GOT back to Virginia at the end of June, we were greeted by the same damp gray weather that we left behind and which had started towards the end of May. There was so much rain that summer, rivers flooded with regularity. Between the months of June and July, the summer seemed permeated by rain and wetness. It was as if the climate of Florida had suddenly transported itself northward by a couple of states, accompanied by intense, yet short downfalls. One overcast morning I took the dogs for a run that led down the hill from our apartment, over a small creek, and eventually up a steep hill heading to the university. The dogs kept up with me on the jog, albeit with pit stops. Cookie led in front, I was in the middle, and Hershey followed behind.

When we got to the small bridge that went over the creek and connected our neighborhood to the university, we noticed it had washed out due to flooding. Part of the bridge was still functional, but a big chunk from the middle had sunk into the creek and been washed away. Water rushed by with an intensity uncommon for the typically tranquil stream, and the small pedestrian bridge hadn't really stood a chance facing the torrent that now came racing through. Fallen tree limbs were clogged underneath and made a makeshift beaver dam. Two men a little older than me had driven down to see the badly-damaged bridge and stood to the side of the flooded creek.

"I haven't seen it this flooded in a long time," one of the men said.

"Don't you remember years ago when it got worse?" the other replied.

"Yeah, it probably won't get like that though."

At this point I was curious. I interjected and asked them how high it had been before. The current river level seemed pretty high to me, and I couldn't imagine it being any higher.

"You see those trees over there?" one guy said, pointing to some tall maple trees close by. "One time back in the '80s the creek got as high as this." He pointed to a spot about fifteen feet up one of the trees.

I had a hard time believing what he said. If what he said were true, it meant the creek would have been a huge river, displacing the area where we stood and quite a ways back. I suppose that could have been the case two hundred years ago, but not thirty. But the story made for good conversation—like an old wives' tale. Nevertheless, the two men and I were in awe of mother nature, and seeing the raging creek gave me trepidation.

When I came back from the jog (I had somehow cautiously circumnavigated the bridge just enough to cross and come back), I had to check the dogs for ticks. Rachel was terrified of ticks and after the time she found some on the dogs and even one in our bed, she was adamant about checking them after each run. Even when I was careful with the dogs and avoided possible grassy danger areas, they would still occasionally end up with a tick on their stomach or one nestled in their ear. This time, at least, the dogs and our bed were safe. With the inspection over and her fears subsided, Rachel showed me something she brought in from the balcony of our back deck.

"Look at this plant," she said while holding the pot of basil she had brought in. The leaves were drooping and the color had turned to a paler shade of green. "This is like, my third try and they keep dying. I just want to make pesto from scratch but these plants are depressing." She greeted each of the dogs to cheer herself up. "Hi Cookie, how was your walk?!" she asked the wiggly, excited, skinny pup.

Our small balcony behind the sliding glass door had a small brick ledge for plants, but because it was a covered balcony, it only got sunlight in the early morning. Before noon, the light would be gone and the basil would be on its own.

"Did you water it enough?" I asked her.

"Yes, I'm pretty sure. What do you think I should do?" she countered with sad eyes. "I'm a plant killer."

"I can try and take care of it. But I have to admit, I don't have a green thumb."

I spent some time trying to nurse the plant back to health: I moved it to a location farther on the ledge, hoping it would get more sun; I watered it a little more, thinking that the humidity and heat were the culprits. Eventually, I surrendered—nothing worked. The location wasn't good for growing—not enough light, and too much heat.

The plant reminded me of my birthday gift from her that year—something I had used on the same balcony. She had tried to keep it a surprise and put it out of sight in her closet. As I lay in bed one warm morning that May, I attempted to ask her what the box was. I wondered about possible gifts a middle-aged man might receive.

"Is it a tie?" I asked.

"No," she said.

"Is it clothes?" I asked again.

"I'm not gonna tell you," she said, holding back a smile.

"Is it a grill?"

Rachel burst out laughing. She still wouldn't say what it was, but I think I had a general idea. The first time I had used the grill was earlier that June, when a friend visited from Washington D.C. The flames had shot up from the briquettes and nearly reached the balcony's ceiling. I could see the fire from inside our apartment as I waited on the other side of the sliding glass door. It provided a sense of comfort to know that I could make a fire outside, long after the weather was too warm to use our fireplace. The flames seemed to provide reassurance and strength. The power and virility of the red-and-yellow blaze was something it seemed I could manage, and that also gave me a sense of stability, albeit a false one.

There was a dual nature to the ascending fire because so much heat can also invoke danger and caution. Occasionally while I was cooking, smoke would fill the balcony and I would worry the smoke alarm would go off. The alarm usually went off when we cooked inside—it was fairly sensitive to any kind of meat cooked in a frying pan or anything that spilled over in the oven. But it never went off for the most dangerous threat of a giant flame shooting up out of the grill on our back patio.

Around the Fourth of July, Rachel traveled to Los Angeles to work as a clinician/educator for the L.A. Philharmonic. I drove her to the airport early that morning and to no surprise, it was raining. The rain came down with violence, and water rushed next to the curbs like small rivers. It was the type of rain that made it a little scary to drive since visibility was low and there was the possibility of hydroplaning. My hands gripped the wheel tightly and both of us were fairly silent, normal for how early it was. But that morning, the silence was more due to the fact our marriage was in jeopardy. The radio was playing (whatever station first came on), and as we got closer to the airport an old song came on with some crooner singing, "It's over/It's over." The irony was not lost on either of us and the song became unbearable after we initially tried to ignore it. I turned off the radio, since it seemed like it was mocking us.

When I dropped her off, I gave her a hug and a kiss and told her I loved her and would miss her. That exchange would be normal under most circumstances and for most couples—for us, it masked some underlying issues. Rachel most likely felt the hug and kiss weren't sincere, and that somehow nullified any positive effects of the goodbye. My family upbringing made it so that most of my hugs and goodbye exchanges were stilted or awkward. Too much excitement was unsettling and too much emotion wasn't to be trusted. Everything was always in moderation in our family dynamic.

Sometimes I didn't kiss her goodbye—it was just a hug. I was always trying to get by with showing as little emotion as possible, and I would definitely hear about it when she got to her destination, because I was in a state of perpetually proving myself—proving I did love her and that she was important to me.

The song that played on the radio on our trip to the airport was exactly the kind of music my grandparents on my mother's side used to listen to. The radio program was called "Music of Yesteryear," and it had provided the soundtrack to many of our family gatherings while we played cards or board games. Thinking about them on the way back home made me recall the time my grandmother passed away unexpectedly in her sleep in 1997. She was the no-nonsense one in the family and she had a way of seeing through people's facades, including my own. When she passed, we lost the quick-witted matriarch who would beat you soundly in a game of pinochle while giving you a wink. My mother asked me to play trumpet at her funeral that fall and right before I was about to play, the pastor said I didn't have to perform if I didn't want to. My mother agreed. For some reason though, I decided to be brave. Someone had to be strong, even though I didn't know what that really meant.

The notes came reluctantly out of my horn and I had to fight back the tears more than once. I wanted to cry and show my grief but I held it in. Both my mom and uncle cried uncontrollably while they greeted people after the funeral, probably remembering all the people and occasions associated with their now-deceased mother, and all the wisdom and support they could no longer turn to. I had never seen them like that before and haven't seen them like that since. In the moment that their grief seeped through their rigid public masks, I was learning how to form my own.

When I got home I took a quick snooze, the insidious song from the radio still reverberating in my head. As I lay half-asleep on the long white couch in the living room, I reflected on our relationship and thought about the good times, times when we clicked and when we seemed like we were part of the same team. I also remembered anxious moments that I could never forget.

One winter a year after we were married, we took a trip to Aruba with her parents and stayed at a timeshare they owned. On the plane trip down to the island located close to Venezuela, I pulled a small black-and-white news flyer out of the pocket in front of me. It contained some local news stories about Aruba, and one story in particular caught my attention. A small fishing boat recently capsized at sea, and two fishermen had struggled to avoid drowning before they could be rescued. Many hours had already passed when a helicopter miraculously arrived and saved one of the men. The other fisherman clung desperately to a buoy and it seemed he would be saved as well. But just as the helicopter lowered to retrieve him, a shark came up from the depths and attacked. They were able to eventually get him on board, but he died from his wounds on the air ride back to land.

By the time we got to Aruba, the fear of sharks was definitely in the back of my mind. When we got to the resort, we settled in and quickly were in vacation mode. Daily events included walking down the hill from the resort, and crossing a road to get to the beach, where little grass canopies attached to wooden poles provided the last barrier before you were met with endless sand and bright blue water. Early evenings were spent enjoying piña coladas at the resort bar, and later evenings included a visit to the casino or a local restaurant. Eventually, Rachel and I ventured out on our own and took a jeep excursion led by a tour company to the other side of the island. The jeep ride ended at a beach and the trip was extremely bumpy in parts—so bumpy that it seemed the vehicle would topple over several times. I held on tightly to the bar next to me as we slowly meandered down a winding dirt path. The vehicle lurched to one side and pushed its suspension to the brink. Was this normal? Maybe jeeps were supposed to do this. A family from Ohio with two daughters sat across from us, and we made small talk until my anxiety got the best of me and I shut up and held on for dear life. Rachel laughed at me for being scared.

After about ten or fifteen minutes (which felt longer), we finally made it down to our final destination. On one side of the beach there was a cliff, where the guides invited us to jump off into the ocean if we so desired. It was maybe a thirty- or forty-foot drop and nothing I hadn't done before when I was younger. The harder, more dangerous part was swimming to shore once you jumped in. That's why they prefaced their invitation by making sure those who jumped were strong swimmers.

There were three people who were brave enough to jump that day—me and two other guys. The first guy to jump was young, athletic, and not afraid. He went in and had no problem making it to shore. One of the guides was already in the water with a flotation device just in case.

I was next and all of the others crowded around the edge to watch as I waited for the signal to jump in. Rachel filmed my leap of faith on her phone. When the other tour guide to my right gave the signal, I ran a couple steps and leapt into the air feeling a combination of delight and bravery. The thrill of dropping and plunging into the ocean was exhilarating. The water was warm and it gave me comfort as I was suspended in a blue flow of something greater than myself. I easily swam towards the beach and made it about halfway to shore. But then, just as my journey was almost complete, the waves behind me kept coming. I dove under, waited until each wave went by and continued on my way. The problem was that each wave would suck me back out to sea just enough to make me feel like I was fighting a losing battle. I swam and swam, moving my arms and shoulders like a machine, but I quickly got more tired and thought I was going to drown. My arms were now like lead bricks and it was getting harder and harder to find air. I just couldn't make any progress—it got to the point that I became scared and worried if this was it. The first guy on the shore was visible and I tried to wave at him to get his attention. My arm was about as high as it could go, but he didn't notice me. He was looking farther past me in another direction. As anyone caught in a riptide or snared by powerful waves knows, one can endure quite well in the beginning and you almost feel confident. But over time your resolve and energy is eroded and you succumb to nature's will. Lucky for me, as I continued to wave, my feet were now somehow touching bottom. I could get up and walk, it was just that my body was done. It was hard to move and I was breathing heavily for quite some time. As I sat down on shore, I felt like I had dodged a bullet. Nobody knew my predicament because it seemed like I was fine, and truth be told, the third guy that went in (the tattooed father from Cleveland, Ohio, who had sat across from me in the jeep) had more problems than me and had to be rescued by the guide. At the same time I was practically drowning, the father behind me was actually in worse shape and all attention had been on him. He must've been pushed out of the channel by the same waves sucking me back out little by little. Rachel finally came up to where I was sitting and was surprised by my condition.

"I almost died," I told her.

"Really? It didn't look like it."

"Yeah, I'm never doing that again," I said as I spat out saltwater.

"Are you OK? Should I get you some water?" she said, a little more concerned.

"No, I just need to sit here for awhile. It's hard to move." I suppose a person can be so good at always being the same on the outside that people don't notice when things are wrong. I didn't look like I needed help because I was ashamed to flail my arms and ask for it—even at the point of drowning. Both Rachel and I were similar in that regard. We thought we were strong. The current underneath was stronger.

After I woke up from the short nap, I took the dogs outside for a walk in the backyard. It was now a sunny day and the rain had stopped completely. As I looked up in the sky I could see Rachel's plane in the air as it left our small town. There was the faint noise of the engine and a tiny white metal bird moving westward. I hoped she would get to her destination safely and wondered if we could navigate the current turmoil in our relationship, or if there was another wave about to engulf me.

Chapter 16
Closer to the Edge

Afflictions point to Gods; Gods reach us through afflictions.
—James Hillman, Psychologist

I APOLOGIZED TO RACHEL in June. I apologized to Rachel in July. I sent her a dozen red roses in a vase with a box of chocolates, since roses were her favorite flower. When the package arrived at her hotel in L.A., the vase was broken.

"Why did you wait so long to send them?" she texted.

During the course of our time together, I would bring home flowers for Rachel. Sometimes I would buy a rose at the store. Sometimes I would bring home beautiful centerpieces from the wedding gig I played that weekend. But I had never bought a dozen red roses. It was too expensive. Consequently, she called me out.

"First time I got that many, which was nice. I was just upset that it took 7 years and infidelity…Before, it was like 1 rose. I wasn't worth a dozen…"

"I didn't know that you would think that. Of course you aren't just worth one rose," I replied.

After she came back from the music festival, there was more apologizing to do. It was hot and sticky outside and the sun was shining. Our apartment was cool but also somehow stifling. The air was thick with tension because her mother was in town to help us out with the dogs and console Rachel in her vulnerable state. Since we were supposed to go to Alaska, Rachel's mother had agreed to help out and stay at our apartment while we were gone. Before we went on the trip however, there needed to be a lot of reckoning. Even a day or two before we left, we still weren't sure we should go.

At that point I had to talk with both Rachel and her mother about the betrayal. It should have been something only between us, but that didn't reflect the relationship she had with her mother. They were in the bedroom packing for a possible trip and as usual, Rachel didn't know what to pack. The door to our bedroom was closed. Rachel periodically came out into the living room to chat or give me an update on what was happening. At first, she didn't want me to go into the bedroom, probably because her mother was upset.

But I knew I had to own up to my mistake so I went in and apologized to both of them. The remorse brought tears to my eyes.

"I want to say that I'm sorry for my actions and sorry for what happened. I know you're hurt and probably think less of me," I said looking first at Rachel and then somewhere in between her and her mother.

As I spoke, Rachel continued to arrange clothes in her closet. As she listened to me, I couldn't read her emotions because she was too busy trying to figure out my own. Rachel's mother was sitting on the floor on the other side of the bed with a suitcase in front of her and a bunch of clothes. I think she appreciated my apology—almost more than Rachel. When I was finished speaking, her mom told me something about religion and owning our sins.

"If you two really love each other, you'll get through this," she added, providing a little bit of hope in our confused state.

I think if I had given Rachel an apology every week like the one I gave in July she would have been in a better place. I didn't though. I assumed that one apology was enough and that we should be able to move on. With someone like Rachel, the healing process takes more time. Rebuilding trust in any relationship takes time, but I thought it was going to be easier. She told me later that she thought I didn't receive enough punishment for what I did; she thought that I had come away with everything not learning my lesson.

There were a couple times when the Alaska trip was almost canceled. It would have been too much under the circumstances and the $900 cancellation fee was a lot, but not unreasonable considering everything going on. But each time I got on the phone, Rachel came over and begged me to wait.

"No, wait. Let's think about this," she said once with a teary-eyed look on her face.

She didn't want to miss out on something she had never experienced. She also was concerned about the cancellation fee. I suppose she mainly wasn't sure about the trip because she thought it would all be for naught if we came back and separated. How can you go on a trip with someone when you're not even sure you'll be together in a couple weeks?

I decided that we should just enjoy the trip and deal with our issues when we got back. Maybe somehow the trip would be magical and we would be in a better place upon our return. Eventually, we decided to go. We had a stopover in Portland, where my sister lived, and arranged a quick visit to see her and her family and my parents, who were visiting as well, before heading over to Anchorage.

Rachel wanted some kind of reconciliation or acknowledgement from my family about my betrayal, even though it was an issue between ourselves. I accepted her idea because maybe it could be a moment of opening up dialogue in my family—an emotional territory we don't normally encounter. I had thoughts of having some kind of small family conference, but it's just not the type of thing that happens easily in a family not accustomed to sharing personal things as a group. The courage to bring it up was difficult to summon—only once when we met my sister for lunch did it surface, and even then the issue was quickly glossed over. Rachel was looking for some kind of intervention and when all was said and done, it seemed like a missed opportunity—not because bringing up our personal issues in front of them was advantageous, but because it was the kind of thing we needed to talk about in order to break through our own shell as a family.

The first evening of our visit, we went to meet a mutual friend from Chicago at a downtown brewery. The meet-up went well with both of us pleased to see a familiar face—we stood in the sun on the rooftop of the brewery and told him we were on our way to Alaska and he later told us about how he had acclimated to the town of Portlandia. After about three beers, it was time to go. My brother-in-law came to pick us up and take us back to my sister's home in neighboring Vancouver. Rachel was doing well but had started to take some potshots at me.

"It's great to talk with someone who gets excited about trumpet pedagogy!" she had said to our friend. "Greg doesn't get excited about anything."

Our drive back was mostly quiet. The lights of the city and the cool Pacific Northwest air surrounded us, providing a little bit of comfort after our long journey that day.

"There were a lot of people at that place," my brother-in-law said.

"Yeah, it seemed like a popular spot," I replied from the back seat. "It was probably time to go though. Those beers were strong."

"I wasn't ready," Rachel said, sitting in the front passenger seat. "I wanted to stay longer."

"Well, I don't think anything good would've happened if we stayed," I replied with a chuckle.

Rachel turned around and gave me an evil stare, trying to elicit an argument. I immediately recognized the situation and evaded any confrontation. When we got to my sister's place, it was late and time to go to bed. My parents were watching TV in a room adjacent to ours, which didn't give us a lot of privacy. As soon as we got into the room and closed the door Rachel wanted to talk about something. Her eyes fixated on me and her tone of voice was combative—she demanded that I engage with her. I could tell she wasn't in a state of mind where we could have a productive conversation.

"We can talk, but let me get ready for bed first," I told her as I flossed my teeth.

I was dead tired from traveling all day and hanging out, and needed to at least unwind before we got into some kind of deep argument. She thought I was stonewalling and stalling, which I was. Past experiences taught me a fight was looming and I still didn't have the skills to head off the impending storm. Luckily, she had some semblance of patience, so she went into another room of the house and called her mother.

Twenty minutes passed and Rachel came back into the room. I was lying on the hide-a-bed, resting and waiting for her, eyes closed. When she saw I wasn't alert and ready to talk with her she became irate. Her look said it all—lips tense and slightly protruded, eyes intently fixated on me yet not quite focused at the same time. She approached me and spoke in a voice much louder than appropriate for the time of night.

"Rachel, I am listening to you. What do you want to talk about?" I said. But I was still lying down in a state somewhere between resting and awake. This pushed Rachel more over the edge. She sat next to me on the bed with rage building up and at this point tried to engage with me in a sexual way, seeing that I wasn't responding.

Somehow the conversation got steered towards the girl in the email. Rachel wanted to know the full truth. What did I do with this girl? How did it happen? What did she look like? What really upset Rachel at this point was the fact I had brought a condom with me when I met up with that girl. She had discovered this a week or so prior after finding some I had long forgotten about in my trumpet case. Of course her next question was if I had them when I met the girl.

Unfortunately for me, I couldn't answer the following question. It was perplexing to me why she wanted to know something so trivial, but in those moments, perhaps nothing is trivial for the person on the other end. She desperately needed the truth and was going to get it somehow.

The next thing I knew Rachel was on top of me, spitting in my face, and hitting me.

"Where did you get the condom from?" she half yelled.

"I don't know," I told her. An uneasiness settled into my soul.

"Why don't you know?" she asked as her voice became louder.

"I don't know. I don't remember."

She immediately became angrier. I desperately tried to crawl into my shell and hide, but there was no shell to crawl into. I sat there and took it. Her punches came down in a staggered fashion, so much so that the worst part was not knowing when to block the next one. Her pale look became a more ghostly white, her eyes became a little darker. But it was more than Rachel's appearance that changed that night. In that moment when she was on top of me, she was no longer somebody I recognized. If she was battling her demon inside, that demon had taken over and she had crossed a threshold to a hidden part of herself.

For some reason, at that moment, Rachel called her mother back. Now, for probably the first time, her mother witnessed the current state her daughter was in. Rachel told her mother I wasn't telling the truth, that I wasn't telling her where I got the condom. Her mother became scared and tried to talk her down. She almost booked a flight home for Rachel right then and there. Eventually, things died down, but it wasn't until Rachel broke down and cried. That was the release that usually brought her back down from the hysteria. She fell asleep, all of her energy unleashed. She would be her regular self again in the morning. I, however, couldn't sleep. The room was spinning. My head was in a fog and it was like I was in another dimension. I couldn't process what had just happened, couldn't process what I just experienced. I was scared for myself, scared for Rachel, scared for the future. The fear came from seeing her in a way I had never seen her, only once maybe when she Skyped me from Japan while drunk, years ago. Her eyes during that call were out of focus and had a mind of their own. This time, she was again controlled by something else, only it just wasn't her. Even during the knife incident she was still somewhat of her recognizable self. This time, she was displaying an uncontrollable rage from deeper within. I thought back to my Tootsie Roll Pop theory and wondered if her shell was completely gone. Maybe she was at the mercy of that which came from within.

There would be a lot of conversations the next day—conversations with Rachel, conversations with my father and conversations with her mother. The sun was shining and the weather was nearly perfect. Rachel and I took a walk around the idyllic suburban neighborhood and held hands while discussing our future. Each house and front yard looked like something from the magazine *Better Homes and Gardens* and each provided a reminder of the place we aspired to live in but remained outside our grasp. Every front yard we passed was cut just right, each bush and tree trimmed to the appropriate size. She was quiet for most of the walk and while it was a conversation she'd had many times in her life, this time was more serious because while there were many previous times she had to deal with the ramifications of an outburst, this time her soul was now on the line. Rachel was very close to going back to Virginia. Her mother thought she really needed a break, a break from me and a break from my family. I would stay with my family and decompress if she went back. The trip to Alaska would of course be canceled, but I didn't mind all that much.

My opinion was that we could continue on to Alaska only if she thought she could control her drinking and not put herself in similar situations. From her point of view, I can only imagine that she was in one of the toughest spots in her life—trying to stand up for herself while knowing at the same time she caused harm in doing so; needing to make sense of our relationship when it was the last thing she could hold on to. Ultimately, we were torn between taking a big step backwards in our relationship, or trying to press on.

When we came back from the walk we were still as confused as when we started. The decision to stay or leave kept going back and forth until finally, at the end of the day, we decided to continue the trip. We decided to keep going. Neither her parents, nor Rachel and I, knew what we were dealing with. My family only knew we were having marriage difficulties and they understood a few of the details. They were not aware of anything else, any of the mental issues or dangerous situations we were dealing with—only Rachel's mother had a glimpse of that in the brief phone call. What lay partially hidden underneath was again covered up—as if time would be a remedy.

Chapter 17
Cruise

Only as we learn to distinguish ourselves from our shadow by recognising its reality as part of our nature, and only if we keep this insight persistently in mind, can our confrontation with the other pairs of the psychic opposites be successful.

—Jolande Jacobi, Psychologist

RACHEL AND I had problems finding people our own age on the Holland America Noordam ship. This was decidedly not a popular summer activity for people in their twenties or thirties (or even forties). One evening towards the end of the cruise, Rachel and I were at a dimly lit bar next to one of the music stages where musicians tended to hang out. The absence of light cloaked its surroundings with an aura of mystery and magic, like turning out the lights before blowing out the candles on a birthday cake. Somehow Rachel knew or had connections with one of the classical musical acts performing on the ship, and so we would spend our time in that area chatting with those musicians or other people who looked our age. At the bar, there happened to be four guys in their late twenties or early thirties hanging out, mostly from the Milwaukee area. Two sat to the right of us and the other two stood behind them, making casual conversation and joking around. Their faces displayed a mix of Midwestern earnestness and playful mischievousness. After a moment, when their conversation about their excursion that day intermingled with ours, Rachel immediately tried to chat with one of the thoughtful-looking guys who was standing.

"So how do you all know each other?" she asked.

"I'm just here with my grandparents. I met these guys a couple days ago," the guy said after taking a drink.

"Oh, cool. Yeah, there's not many young people on this cruise," she said.

"Uhhh, nope," was his reply.

"So what do you do for a living?" she asked.

"Well, I'm studying medicine, gonna become a doctor—just not sure which kind yet."

"Very cool. Greg's sister is a doctor. This is my husband Greg, by the way.

"Nice to meet you."

"Likewise," I replied.

"So what kinds of medicine are you currently studying?" Rachel asked.

"Um, I'm doing my rotations. I started off with pediatrics, then went to internal medicine, and now I'm in family medicine. I have dermatology left."

"Nice, well what kind do you prefer best?"

"I'm not really sure to be honest."

"Well, tell me this: what was a time you remember being most happy as a doctor? Or what made you want to go into medicine?"

"Oh, man. That's a tough question. I suppose when I participated in a program that sent students studying medicine to some underdeveloped parts of the world. I got sent to Haiti. I enjoyed it though. I was working a lot with kids and educating them on health stuff."

"So what kind of medicine would that be? Pediatrics?"

"Yeah, could be. But I might be interested in doing something like Doctors without Borders. I don't know. It's tough."

"You should do that then! That seems like it could be a good fit."

Keep in mind, conversations like these with Rachel could go on for hours. Also keep in mind the more she connected with people, the more animated she got. As a result, Rachel was now the center of attention at the bar. All the guys were crowded around her as she quizzed their friend. It was like a master class on connecting, and she was the professor with eager students awaiting where the conversation would go next. Eventually, she helped the medical student by encouraging him to reflect more on his future career choice. Everyone was pleased to be talking about something meaningful and not engaging in mundane small talk.

Rachel proceeded to talk to the guy who stood just behind the medical student. She found out he was engaged to be married and tossed him a full volley of questions to find out if he was ready. Rachel was in the zone. She probably would have continued to connect in a meaningful way with everybody at the bar that night had it not been for the alcohol. By this time her game was starting to slip and she resorted to again venting relationship wounds in public. She let out an inappropriate comment about how I cheated on her and everyone realized the show was over. They closed their tabs.

"Why are you telling me this?" was the youngest guy's response. He seemed confused and disappointed, like he couldn't understand how things could go from light to dark so quickly. I immediately started in on damage control before we headed back to our room— me with a bruised ego, and her with a puzzled-but-pleased look, not quite registering that she had overstepped her bounds.

Earlier that day we had arrived at Juneau and hopped on an excursion to go whale watching. We were both excited to explore Alaska and its wildlife, since there's something about traveling such a long distance for vacation, and then traveling just a little bit more to experience a place so remote that you feel you might never return. It becomes a sacred place, one kindred to your soul.

Our small tour group consisted of about ten people and the weather that day was cool and cloudy. The boat carried us through Gastineau Channel, with huge peaks on either side of us. It didn't take us much time to enter Fritz Cove, and then we were out in the open water. The humpback whales were supposedly over to our right in Auke Bay, so we sped over there, and by this time the water was a little more choppy. The boat bounced up and down, and at that speed, my nerves got the best of me. "What if our boat hits a whale?" I wondered. I held Rachel's hand and she could sense I was nervous. It amused her that my nerves were again getting the best of me, just like our rafting trip in Montana and just like the jeep ride in Aruba. This time, with the sound of the boat and wind hindering conversation, she just smiled in acknowledgment.

By the time we got to Auke Bay, the sky was now partially sunny. The water was calmer and we were surrounded by an expanse of blue, coupled with patches of green—so many vibrant colors that it was like feeling the spirit of the world. The boat slowed down and crept along, waiting for a sighting.

"Over there!" someone shouted. You could see just a fin, but it was something to behold. The black triangle plunged back into the water with grace and force. That there could be such an awe-inspiring presence beneath us and around us was exhilarating.

The next sighting was closer. We eventually got within about fifty meters of the massive, dark-colored mammal, and this time you could see more of the back poking out of the water—a black presence slowly rose up to investigate its surroundings and went back under. Our tour boat was like a man alone on the sea of the world, and the whale represented a shadowy other. I again wondered, What happens if the whale decides to pop up underneath our boat? Has that ever happened? We were ten people strong and our boat was sturdy. Still, we would be no match for such a behemoth rising from the depths.

Not much was said between the folks in our tour, but there was a feeling of admiration and respect for the sacred place we now occupied. When we couldn't spot any more whales, we headed closer to the shore. Off in the distance, we could see an expanse of pine trees that crept almost right up to the water. The tour guide spoke to us:

"All right, we need some volunteers to pull some crab traps," he said. Rachel looked at me.

"You should do it," I said.

"Really? Do you want to come with me?" she asked.

"Nah, I think they already have enough people," I replied.

She went to the front of the boat with one or two others and had to don some black protective gloves to make sure her hands didn't get dirty. I snapped a photo of her to embarrass her, and she had one of those smiles that children get when they are about to do something fun but don't know what. Her eyes were tired and a little puffy—the result of getting up early for our excursion and the result of probably thinking too much about our relationship.

The crab traps were cages located at the bottom of the ocean, just in front of our boat. The volunteers were there to watch the guide dislodge the cages from the water and place them onboard, in the hopes of seeing and maybe holding a crab. They were also there to help set the traps with new bait.

The guide slowly pulled up a crab pot, and even though he warned that there might not be anything in it, people were still eager to see what would appear from the depths below. I couldn't really see what was happening from my vantage point in the back of the boat. The others at the front, including Rachel, peered at the dripping cage and it was apparent nothing was inside. One would have thought that at least a solitary crab might have been inside, or perhaps a small, shiny fish of some Alaskan variety. But there was nothing.

"All right, we need a volunteer to help add new bait to this trap," said the guide.

"I'll do it," Rachel agreed wholeheartedly.

She reached into a large, plastic white bucket and with her long black gloves, placed something mysterious inside the crab pot. She repeated this action several times.

When she finished, she removed her gloves and returned to the back of the boat with a pleased look on her face.

"OK, hopefully that'll make sure we got something in those traps next time we return," said the guide.

"What did you put inside the trap?" I asked her.

"Oh, nothing," she replied.

"What do you mean, nothing?"

Rachel seemed amused about something, like she was keeping a secret. By the time the boat got going and the wind started to whip around us, it became too noisy again to talk. I never got an answer out of her.

How do you lure something out of its home, into a trap, and hope that it will eventually appear? Especially when that something is buried deep below. Any regular crab or fish is extremely small, alone and unique—the sea is great and vast. The guides thought they were in the right spot, but maybe the crab traps weren't in the right place. I imagined that the Native Americans who maybe fished for crabs had more wisdom in finding them. I still don't know what Rachel put in the trap that day, but even more curious is why she didn't tell me. I'm sure whatever it was, she believed that the ocean would eventually produce, and there would be fresh bounty from the revered bottom of Auke Bay.

A day or so later we found ourselves strolling through downtown Ketchikan. We ate lunch at a nearby seafood restaurant called the Alaska Fish House, and found a bus to go up the hill and visit the Totem Heritage Center. Part of our meandering was interrupted by Rachel talking to her mom on the phone about how our relationship was doing.

"Mom, I don't know," she said in response to her mom's inquiry. She seemed frustrated and would periodically look back at me. Again she mentioned that she wasn't sure and became upset. I stood nearby and remained silent, since I felt like I was still walking on eggshells. "Are things black or are things white?" seemed to be the gist of the conversation—meanwhile I stood close by representing the color gray. After some time, she was able to end the conversation and we continued over to the bus stop.

The Heritage Center was a museum of Native Americans who used to live in the area, and while it was something I could get interested in, Rachel took one look inside and turned the other direction to walk back out. The sun was shining and the weather was a perfect seventy degrees, so we ventured over to the nearby park and held hands as we walked through the small, picturesque spot of green that featured about everything a park should have—tall, shady evergreen trees, a small creek, lots of grass and bushes, and a small walkway through the middle of it all. There was also a fish hatchery that you could walk by, so we continued over there and didn't say much the entire time. I felt her hand in mine and tried to think of what to say and tried to gauge her mood. It seemed like the perfect romantic walk, but it also almost seemed like spending time with someone before you know they have to go back somewhere else—like we were just killing time or marching in place.

Her hand was much smaller than mine and while at first we grasped each other for pleasure, after awhile we just held onto each other because that was all there was to hold onto. In some ways, it was like my first day of kindergarten, when I left my mother's company for the first time. I held her hand while we walked up the street from our house to the school. We walked by the house with the annoying chihuahua called Pepsi, we walked by my friends' houses, and we walked by the house that had the petrified rocks near the driveway (I later stole one, and it remained a doorstop in our own home for years). I felt scared since I didn't understand why she couldn't come with me inside the school, and I later cried those first couple days after being separated the first time. I had to get all the tears out before I could continue with the day, and so it was really my first experience with emotional pain and abandonment— the hand I held and the feeling of closeness to another that I realized was only temporary. Intimacy has a price, and the price you pay for love is something that is traded in for pain later down the road.

Later that week during our time at sea, I played a couple poker tournaments, came in first and second place, and won several hundred dollars. On the surface I probably seemed like normal, but deep down I was excited because I had never won a poker tournament in any type of casino before. I also saw it as a sign of good luck that maybe would carry over into our relationship.

It was Rachel's birthday, so I went to the jewelry store on the ship and picked out some tanzanite earrings she might like. When I came back to the room, Rachel was resting on the bed.

"Guess what? I won the tournament!"

"Really? That's great," she said, turning over.

"Yeah, I also got you something."

I gave her the earrings and thought she would see it as a sign of my love. The thing with Rachel though, was that she didn't wear a lot of jewelry and was very picky about what she wore.

"Oh, that's sweet of you," she said, looking it over with curiosity. "I don't know if I'd wear them though."

"Really? It's not something you'd like?"

"Hmm, they're pretty. I just think it's a waste of money since I wouldn't wear them much."

"Well, we can go return them and maybe find something you like," I said, hoping she would eventually accept my gift.

We wandered over to the jewelry store and looked at what they had to offer, but a lot of it was too expensive—it was difficult to find something priced at a couple hundred dollars to replace the earrings. In the end, we ended up returning them and the sales associate who had helped me first pick out the gift gave Rachel a curious look.

She frequently made me feel like my romantic efforts weren't good enough and this was one of those times. This time, she was trying to be practical while I was trying to be romantic. On the surface I probably seemed like I was fine, but deep down I felt rejected and disappointed. I wondered how someone who cared so much about intimacy and being close could also seemingly reject that same affection when it was presented to her. It made me want to stop trying. What if the thing Rachel and I both thought, but didn't consciously recognize, was that only pain creates intimacy? That we couldn't reach each other because we were too busy unconsciously confirming each other's unworthiness.

When we got back from the Alaska trip, we had a day layover in Seattle before heading back to Virginia. We passed time that afternoon by going to a movie Rachel wanted to see. My parents drove us to the nearby shopping mall in Tukwila, and we all watched a newly awarded documentary entitled *Three Identical Strangers*. It chronicled the story of identical triplets, separated at birth for the purposes of a psychological study. The movie started off as a fascinating tale of three long-lost brothers who randomly reconnected later in life and discovered all of the things they had in common. But a little over halfway through, the story took a dark turn and it was revealed that there was a history of mental health issues. The documentary asked the question, "Which is more influential: nature or nurture?" It also asked: "How does environment shape us, and to what extent did the psychological study affect their mental health?" One of the brothers took his life after bouts with manic depression.

As we got up to leave the theater, Rachel turned and exited our row of seats to the left. My parents and I exited to the right. No words were exchanged; we were still under the spell of what we had watched. We shuffled up the aisle and Rachel glanced over at us with a pensive look on her face before disappearing through a different exit. We waited for her to reappear for quite some time and she eventually surfaced again after visiting the restroom. I wondered why she went her separate way without saying anything, but maybe I was overthinking things.

The movie made me recall a random fight we had in our apartment before the Alaska trip. At some point I left our apartment to blow off steam. I went to a nearby bar for a drink and was gone for maybe fifty minutes. As I came back and headed up the hill to our apartment, Rachel called me, wondering where I was. I didn't answer because I was almost home. In the next several minutes and in her frustration at being abandoned, Rachel reverted again to self-harm. There was no evidence when I got home because I arrived before she got very far. She also didn't let on that anything had happened. But a day later I asked her what the imprint was on her neck. There was a faint red mark and it looked like it came from wearing a necklace. She revealed it came from something she used to choke herself. I didn't know what to say and I couldn't comprehend her words. I was glad I came home when I did.

What do you do when someone hands you the dark part of their soul and presents it as if it is a normal side of themselves? Rachel was past issues of self-harm, but that summer was a relapse into the raging current that ran deep within her. The current was made stronger still by opening up a dam that held back my own issues.

It seemed like every time we negotiated a crisis that summer, we would arrive at a good point. We talked, reconciled, explained, and we would be on good terms for a little while. Then, Rachel would find something on my computer or phone to confront me with—things I had long forgotten about. When she revealed the cause of the imprint on her neck, we were back on good terms, and things were better between us. It was similar to times when she cut herself in the beginning of our relationship, and this was far less damaging or lasting than those cuts. Unfortunately, while her self-harm normally happened when I was around—this was a case where it happened when I wasn't there.

Chapter 18
Darkness in August

Can I ever be comfortable with him and trust him?—He says he just wants to start over, but is that even psychologically possible?—If he stops this, what is the next thing going to be? Is he going to take me down with him?—Would separation be good for our relationship and me?—How do I understand a person that would be in a relationship without caring?

ON AUGUST 1ST, the proactive and problem-solving side of Rachel tried to think through her dilemma and wrote down her thoughts about the predicament. She was still in a searching mode because within the past few days, she had somehow managed to track down the Venezuelan girl via social media (information I didn't have and couldn't even dig up). She compared herself to exacerbate her insecurities, contacted her, and verified that everything I told her was correct. She was like a lawyer collecting evidence and making a case—a case against herself more than a case against me, because at the same time that she tried to discover every disloyal moment from my past, she also crept into the dirtiest corners of her own value and self-worth. By August 1st, she had all the information she thought she needed.

By August 3rd, she reverted back to the other radical side of herself. It was a Friday and I told Rachel I was thinking about sitting in with a band who had a gig that night at a local music venue, but hadn't made up my mind. When we were sitting on the couch that

warm muggy evening, Rachel increasingly became more combative and engaged me in a way that seemed like she wanted a fight.
Consequently, perhaps it was a good idea to leave the house and
prevent further bickering. I told her I was going there to play, not
socialize, and I wouldn't be that long. She consented, albeit with
a little hesitation. While I played downtown at the bar, she called
her mom, who convinced her that her husband shouldn't leave her
home alone on a Friday night.

So Rachel made herself a drink, and prepared to go out on the
town in search of her husband. She rode in an Uber and when she
got there, I'll admit I was a little afraid. She was personable with
everyone at the bar while I was playing, but also had arrived there
like a heat-seeking missile ready to confront its target. I finished
playing and went to the bar, where she had been chatting and making herself at home. I tried to be casual with her and to be social,
but she was basically there to continue the fight she had started
back at the apartment. At that point, it became my job to get both
of us out of there as quickly as possible. It involved a lot of leading
and baiting and there were times when she wanted to have it out
right then and there. We left the bar somehow, and were standing
in the plaza area, otherwise known as the downtown mall.

She touched my cheek and as she caressed it, she said to me,
"You're a psychopath. How does it feel to be a psychopath?"

An elderly lady came up to us and pleaded with us in a shaky
tone of voice.

"Please be nice to each other. You two ought to be kind to each
other."

We both ignored the lady. I managed to lead Rachel back to the
car and we drove home. No punches were thrown in the car this
time, though the atmosphere was electric. I used every phrase and
trick in the book I had learned up to that point to keep her at bay.

When we came back home Rachel continued drinking and I
tried to go to bed. Our apartment seemed to shrink as there seemed
to be no place to escape or evade her. I tried to convince her it
was time to go to bed. She was having none of it. She continued

to press me and press me, and the angrier she got, the more distant I became. The next thing I knew, she was spitting in my face. Then she was hitting me. I tried to keep her away by holding her wrists. She tried to tackle me and ended up charging me several times. I eventually positioned myself like a wrestler with two legs firmly planted on the ground, my right leg in front of the left. I became like a tree so that I would be able to use my size to repel any charge. Our dog Hershey came into the room with an eagerness to ascertain the situation. We locked eyes and I'll never forget the questioning, concerned look he had on his face. He seemed like he wanted to help us. He seemed to also know there was nothing he could do to help—no way to come in between the two people he loved the most.

Rachel fell back a couple times. I think she fell awkwardly into an end table—something she would not remember but feel the next morning with an unexplained soreness. She pinned me on the couch and started to bite my groin area. Not long after, the hysteria wore off and she broke down crying. She was exhausted and she passed out on the couch. I held her and tucked her in. I felt more like a father now than a husband, just trying to protect her, but it was really too late. An eerie silence had settled in the apartment after the spurt of chaos, and I wondered if the neighbors heard what just happened. I regretted leaving her there on the couch and going to bed, but she needed to sleep it off and I knew she would be better in the morning. It's also hard to feel love and affection for someone who just tried to beat you up. The same feelings of being unloved, being angry and ashamed were now in me; just like they had been in her.

The following day we experienced what I now call the mental illness hangover. She found me in the morning and forced me to have make-up sex, a common occurrence after a blow out. Every time I said no, she persisted—as if she needed it to replace any bad feelings. Later in the day, Rachel was back to her normal self and trying to move on like nothing major happened, but I could tell she felt confused and detached. She was definitely quieter and probably still in a somewhat dark place. I, on the other hand, was emotionally and physically hurt, and trying to get through to her without making her feel bad.

I had to take the car in to get an inspection, so later in the morning Rachel took me back to the garage to pick the car up. We convened afterwards at a local Applebee's (I had a gift card). Rachel ended up getting there first and had to wait ten to fifteen minutes before I arrived.

"How you gonna make this pretty girl wait?" the waitress said as I sat down in the booth across from my wife.

"No, it's fine," Rachel replied, back to her normal, understanding self.

"I was coming from the garage and they took longer to finish up the checkout process," I added.

There was a colorful advertisement on the table. It read "Mucho means more to sip." Apparently at Applebee's they used common Spanish words to sell more drinks, and it was possible to order a "Mucho." I commented to Rachel how ridiculous the advertisement was since technically "más" means more and "mucho" means a lot or many. It just sounded weird to order a "Mucho" because it's like saying you want "an a lot size" for your drink. Since when did "a lot" become a size? Why do things have to be so extreme? The conversation shifted to our issues. Rachel was checked out, indicated by the fact that she was more quiet than usual and not leading any of the conversation. She understood the dire situation we were in but was trying not to feel the hurt.

"Do you think it would be better if we took time apart? I could find a separate apartment for a little while—maybe something month-to-month," I said.

This was the only solution I had. I thought my presence made Rachel act out and that if we took time apart, she could heal and not think about me so much. She said she wasn't sure if it was a good idea.

As we were leaving the restaurant and paying the bill, the proper tip amount would have been eight dollars.

"I can't leave eight dollars for the tip," I told her. "I'm superstitious about the number eight."

Rachel seemed intrigued. "Why are you superstitious?"

"I don't have a good explanation but… the number eight is like a whole, complete number and it makes me feel there's a finality to things. Things are no longer open ended. And, from my experience in bars and restaurants, it seems like I have bad luck anytime I pay an amount that has a number eight in it."

Rachel didn't respond, but her smile made it seem like she was amused. In terms of briefly separating, she would later look online at apartment options for herself that August and thought about it logically, but there was probably the other side of herself that felt the fear of abandonment she dealt with her whole life. Now as an adult mature enough to deal with these issues, she initially went along with the idea of a temporary separation. But while sitting down at the dining room table not long after our visit to Applebees, she asked me about a recent visit to a vacant apartment.

"How was it?" she asked.

"Not good," I replied while standing across from her on the other side of the table. "It was too small and run down. Maybe I'll look at another one later on."

"Are you serious about this?" Her eyes showed a look of concern. "Do you think it's a good idea?"

I looked down at the ground to think. A short moment passed and I looked up at her and then to the right. "It might not even be possible. I don't know what else to do."

"You don't seem upset by it. Why aren't you more upset?"

"Rachel, of course this isn't what I want to do. I'm just looking at places, that's all," I said in a pleading tone of voice.

The reason why I'll always remember the conversation we had that August at Applebee's was that the Wednesday of that following week was August 8th—8-08-18 to be exact. While my superstition around the number 8 didn't extend to dates, it was hard not to note its unusual repetition. On that particular Wednesday, I had work orientation in the morning. I was a new teacher in a new school district, and so I was going through district teacher training and making sure my paperwork was in order. After the partial day of training, I drove home and right as I pulled into the parking lot around 2:30 p.m., I got a call from Rachel.

"Are you serious about working on our marriage?" she asked.

I was perplexed why that would be the first thing out of her mouth. "Why?" I asked.

"I was on your computer and found the picture of a girl you clicked on—the one from Facebook."

I didn't know what she was talking about. She made a habit that summer of digging up stuff on my computer and this instance was no different. Usually it was something that seemed inconsequential to me or something I had long forgotten about. When I went inside to see what she was talking about, she was sitting in front of my computer in the back bedroom. She showed me the picture of a girl I had clicked on. It was the photo of some fake friend request, the kind I normally delete or ignore. But the girl's photo that morning looked familiar for some reason so I decided to click on it. She was attractive so Rachel maybe felt threatened. She wanted to know why I would be interested in something like that if I was serious about fixing our marriage.

What followed was a very frustrating conversation. I was frustrated because it seemed like she was looking for reasons to divide us. Her constant computer digging pushed my patience to the brink.

"If you really want to find something, look in my photos folder," I said. "You can probably find something in there if you want to just make up stuff."

There was nothing in there of course, but I wanted her to realize how crazy it was to search through someone's computer, grasping at straws until you find something you don't like.

"You're just looking for reasons to get a divorce. You don't really love me," I said in disbelief. The hardest part for me in the past year was to see Rachel stop loving me like the way she used to—the way she stopped laughing at my jokes, was more indifferent to my opinions, and found more opportunities to criticize. It seemed like she was in the initial stages of breaking up, and that was something I never thought was possible with her.

I went to the couch in the other room, sat down, and buried my head in my hands. Rachel and I continued to talk a little bit, me sitting on the couch, her standing in the doorway of the other room. We didn't make any progress. It was a frustrating stalemate with both sides confused, and we retreated to the defensive sides of our personalities, rather than confront something in front of us we were too scared to acknowledge. At one point, I said something that she misinterpreted to mean that I did have sex with the Venezuelan girl. I immediately clarified what I meant and tried to make it clear that she didn't just catch me in a revealing moment. For a brief second, she thought she had finally got the information she had been trying to get the whole summer, even if it wasn't the truth. My sincere denial just made her more confused.

Later that day in the same back bedroom, she was practicing and getting ready for her gig rehearsal the next morning. About thirty minutes or so into her practice session she stopped, and I could tell she was crying or was upset. I went into the room and noticed she had written something down in a journal.

"What are you writing?" I asked her.

"I'm a horribly flawed person and nobody can love me. Maybe I should just end my life," she said with tears in her eyes.

"Rachel, that's not true. You can't say that. It's not true." I held her in my arms. I held her until she seemed better. I didn't think she was serious about ending her life because I'd heard her say the same thing various times throughout our relationship—not often, but enough. I also didn't know what else to say because I didn't know how to convince her that the things she was saying weren't true.

"Rachel, I need to meet you halfway," I told her, realizing I hadn't done my part earlier in the day in reaching her emotionally.

"I need to do a better job of meeting you halfway," I told her again.

This seemed to make her feel better. She was no longer crying.

Not much later, I was practicing in the same room, since I had a gig that evening. It was important because my gigs were few and far between those days, and it was a rare opportunity to do some playing. I was too concerned about warming up, coming up with a tune list, and getting to the gig. Regrettably, I never looked down to see what Rachel had written in the journal. I also thought she had told me.

She made a new recipe of turkey meatloaf that evening and thought we were going to eat dinner together before my gig—but at this event, food would be provided, so I left a little before dinnertime and she ate alone. Despite her fragile condition, everything that happened around the time I left and a little bit after was normal. I could tell she was still dealing with the hurt. When she was in the kitchen I passed her, walking through the dining room, headed to the stairs and told her I would be home by 9:45. I was in a rush making sure I wasn't late to my gig. I thought about saying I love you, but instead came out the typical thing I would say instead:

"I'll be thinking about you." She didn't respond and seemed to be thinking about what I said. When I got to the bottom of the stairs, I remembered something I forgot to do.

"Rachel," I said. She shortly appeared at the top of the stairs. "Can you feed the dogs? I forgot." She immediately went about getting their food.

Rachel made the dinner that evening, ate a little bit of it, did the dishes and put everything away. She spent some time that evening researching why her pinky finger suddenly had problems with numbness. She had an appointment with a doctor the following week. Rachel also confirmed that she would be carpooling the next morning to her gig rehearsal located about forty-five minutes away. They were to meet in a grocery store parking lot. Since she was upset, Rachel did what she normally did in those circumstances. She reached out to a couple of friends via text to see if they could chat. One friend replied they could chat the next day or Friday, and the other friend replied late that night that they could chat during the weekend. All of this was normal behavior from Rachel, normal for anyone really. What happened next I still don't know to this day, and I can only hypothesize based on her phone and computer activity. I can only guess that the dark side that had been leading Rachel down a path of no return had finally got the better of her.

Chapter 19
Blindness

*Sometimes we act in order not to see. I may well be actively
doing and taking part in order to avoid knowing what my soul
is doing and what interior person has a stake in the action.*
—James Hillman

THROUGHOUT THE YEAR prior to that second week
of August, we began having trouble seeing things. At one
point, I developed a problem with my eyes and my contact
lenses started to burn. Sometimes I wore them anyway. When I
visited the optometrist, he told me I would need new glasses and
wouldn't be able to wear contacts ever again. I was shocked and
couldn't believe what he said.

"If you want to see, you shouldn't wear contacts. There are
some blood vessels around the cornea that have increased due to
lack of oxygen. If these enter the cornea, it could result in vision
loss or complete blindness," he told me.

On the way home, I immediately called Rachel. I was almost
resigned to my new fate, even though it depressed me.

"No, you need a second opinion. That's crazy! Are you sure you
can trust this guy?" she said.

"I don't know. How can I *not* trust him? But maybe he just
wants me to buy glasses."

"Let me see if I can find an eye doctor here with my insurance,"
she said.

Rachel helped me find another optometrist who gave me a second opinion, and we determined I just needed new contacts. Later, I actually went to another doctor who told me I could wear contacts again, but I would have to wear glasses for several months in order for my eyes to heal from the damage caused earlier. I'd never had problems with my eyes before and was really worried that I might lose part of my vision. My new optometrist instructed me to wipe my eyelids with a special cleaning pad every night before bed and use a heating device to improve blood flow.

The issue of blindness came up again later when Rachel did a master class at the Virginia School for the Deaf and Blind. She worked with the middle school band and helped the new trumpet students learn their instrument. Everything should have been routine since she did that kind of thing a lot, but I got a frantic voicemail from her that day while I was teaching.

"Hey! Can you come pick me up after school? I lost my keys and we can't find them anywhere!" she said.

Luckily, the school wasn't too far from where I worked. I left my own school a little earlier than normal that day and drove by to pick her up. I made my way through the narrow downtown streets of Staunton, and after ascending multiple hills, I ended up at a parking lot next to several large red brick buildings with white pillars. Rachel's red Chevy Aveo was inside the small parking lot, so I waited there for quite some time since she still hadn't appeared from the building. When she finally appeared from the other side of the school campus, I was relieved. By the time she got in the car, I was annoyed for waiting so long.

"Any luck?" I asked before greeting her.

"Hi. No, we'll have to leave my car here. Can you get a locksmith tomorrow to open the car? My spare doesn't open the door."

"Yeah, I guess so—depends on when," I said.

"So, what happened to the keys?" I asked.

"We don't know. They literally just disappeared along with my jacket," she replied. The car ride home was more silent than normal.

"Can't you just be more sympathetic?" she asked at one point. "I had a shitty day and you're not making me feel better."

"Hey, I'm here aren't I? I came to get you."

"Thanks," was her curt response.

The mystery of her keys was solved months later when school got out. After Rachel had already gone through the hassle of getting replacement keys, the school called to inform her that the jacket and keys were hanging inside a student locker. Apparently, one of the students must have picked them up by mistake.

By August 8th, Rachel and I were accustomed to not seeing well and somehow losing something in the process—we lost sight of each other. I spent the majority of that summer trying to restore normalcy or regain stability in the relationship, and it helped prevent me from seeing her true condition. We both wanted to find a remedy for our situation, but how do you keep putting one foot in front of the other if you can't see where you're going? Besides, Rachel couldn't go back to normal.

After texting her friends and responding to a few emails that night, Rachel put away dinner, did the dishes, and drank a little bit of the boxed wine that was on the counter. She next probably took the dogs for a walk. When she came back, she might have decided to go to the gym that was a part of our apartment complex and located just down the hill. The time was 7:54 p.m. and there was still daylight. I can only guess that she went to the gym based on what she was wearing when I came home—some greyish workout clothes and no shoes or socks. 7:54 was also the time stamp on her phone when she left our apartment and went out, or maybe just down the hill. Going to the gym was also something she would have done under normal circumstances. While there, I imagine that Rachel realized she needed to put gas in the car since she would be driving her and a colleague the next morning.

I can only hypothesize that Rachel finished her workout a little earlier than normal and took the car to the local gas station located about ten minutes or so away. While at the gas station, she might have purchased a big bottle of wine at the convenience store (bigger than she normally would get) and drove back home. The time was around 9 p.m. It was getting dark. She received one text from her mother at 9:03 while she was driving home but she didn't open it. At 9:08 she received a text from me as she was arriving at our apartment but didn't open it, maybe because the dogs were barking and she didn't hear the ping. When she got in the apartment, she took off her shoes and socks, because they were left on a bar stool near the kitchen. She set down her purse (with her phone inside) and the bottle of wine on the kitchen table. She got a coffee cup from the cupboard and poured herself a full cup from the boxed wine already in the kitchen. She kept refilling her cup, until the box was almost empty and she needed to open it up and take the bag out to get all that remained. The wine helped Rachel spiral. She went into the bedroom and continued to write in her journal. She continued venting her hurt and pain, but this time it was with a clear intention. She wrote:

> *I'm glad I will be less of an emotional burden for you Greg. The unemotional always win. Congratulations and well done...*
> *At 33 with Herpes and a DUI and my love life track record I don't expect to ever have what I longed for—love—true love...*
> *I don't want to even try to get through this feeling so that's why I am done trying. The only thing that ever mattered to me was falling in love and finding a life partner to share my life with and I couldn't do that. I failed and (I'm) tired of trying.*

She got up, took off her jacket (it had been raining a little outside) and threw it in the closet. She got what she needed from the closet to set things up. She continued to drink the wine. She took a break to write a note to her family saying she loved them and just couldn't face the disappointment of not achieving her goal of finding love. She signed it using her maiden name and proceeded with the act. Maybe she wanted me to find her and save her. Maybe she didn't.

My gig that evening was supposed to end at 9 p.m. As far as I knew, the band would play two sets and be done. When 9 o'clock came, the rest of the band acted as if the gig wasn't over so I was confused. I inquired and found out we were playing three sets and ending at 10 p.m. The bandleader had written down the wrong information in the email he sent me.

I texted Rachel (the one at 9:08): "The gig that was 7-9 PM in the email, is now 7-10. Ugh."

Her Google Timeline History says that 9:09 was when the phone was set down. Maybe she saw the text and didn't click on it—maybe she didn't hear the ping and didn't even see it. Regardless, 9:09 was the last activity on her phone, when she supposedly came back home from wherever she went, came inside and set her stuff down on the kitchen table.

My gig was at a restaurant in downtown Staunton at a place called the Mill Street Grill. That night, as people ate ribs and sandwiches, I played jazz standards with a rhythm section that was a mixture of various ages and abilities. The decor was green and brown with outdated green carpet and thick wood beams in between tables. It seemed like playing in someone's basement.

I awaited her text reply and joined the band gathered at a nearby booth. They all decided to order strawberry shortcake for dessert, though I don't think I joined them. As we were sitting at the table a short lady came and sat down. She had long hair, was heavy set, and soulful. She was also a friend of the band and an amateur singer of sorts. When the waiter came by and served the dessert, the lady started to sing an impromptu song about strawberry shortcake. The song was basically the word strawberry shortcake repeated and accompanied with a theatrical, bluesy melody.

"Straw-berry shortcake," she sang with eyes wide open and a smile. She looked around the table at approving grins from the rest of the band. At the time, it seemed kind of strange, but also humorous in a quirky kind of way. The character Strawberry Shortcake also happened to be one of Rachel's favorite Halloween costumes.

When we had played the last song of the night, I packed up my instruments and had an opportunity to speak to that lady before heading home. I found out she worked for or had some connection to the university.

"Oh, is Rachel the trumpet professor your wife?" she asked me. As she stood in front of me while we briefly chatted and exchanged pleasantries, it seemed like there was something else on her mind. Since it was late and I still hadn't heard back from Rachel, I excused myself.

I called her about halfway home around 10:20 but there was no answer. My immediate thought was maybe she was having a late-night gym session like she had a few nights earlier. Even so, I drove quicker because something didn't seem right. By the time I got home around 10:50 that night, she was already gone. There was a full coffee cup of wine left on the table she didn't need, a strange thing to see since I'd never seen her drink wine in a coffee cup before.

Rachel hung herself in the closet. Next to her limp, suspended body that seemed like a ghost, was a stepladder well within reach if she needed to use it. Her feet almost touched the ground so I assumed she passed out in the position I found her. I couldn't comprehend that she had gone that far and wasn't prepared for what I found that night. While I always thought I was the cause for her suffering and anger, what I didn't understand and couldn't see was that without me around, the pain and violence would still be there. She used it against herself. In her last act on earth, she demanded that the unknown face that had previously ruled her be revealed.

Chapter 20
The Aftermath

It is to the soul one must look for the justification of a suicide.
—James Hillman

ALL THE LIGHTS were on when I got home that night. The window shades were all open. Anyone walking in the backyard who looked up could have seen Rachel and what she had done. Nobody did that I'm aware of. It wasn't possible to see out the windows of our back bedroom at night when the lights were on—only possible to see inside. Rachel's window on the world would have been black that night, much like the dark view she had accumulated that summer.

When I got home, I came up the stairs from our front door and didn't say anything, only listened for the sound of someone's presence. The dogs were on our bed in our bedroom and hadn't rushed to greet me or say hello. There was a feeling that there should have been somebody home, but yet also a feeling that nobody was. When I looked into the bedroom, they finally greeted me with wagging tails, but did not get up. I looked in the kitchen, next the bathroom. As I went to the back bedroom, the door was open just a little. I entered the room and looked just behind the door and saw Rachel suspended, with her head slightly down, eyes wide open, no sign of life. Her feet were not far from the ground, but just enough that they weren't touching anything. Apparently, according to the detective, the scissors she used to cut the rope to the right length were on the futon. I never saw them. There was a stepladder near her body. I immediately got on the stepladder and tried to get her down. She was heavy as I held her up to relieve the tension of the rope on her neck. I couldn't get enough slack to get her down. I also couldn't leave her to go get the scissors, which I thought were in the kitchen.

"What are you doing?" I asked her as dread filled my body. It felt like it was a dream—like it was just another one of those times when she went off the deep end, and I could make things better or I could somehow keep her from going off the cliff.

After what seemed like an eternity, but was probably several minutes, I was able to create enough slack on the rope while still holding her up, and I could pull her off. I held her and took care of her like all the times before when she drank too much and passed out. I took care of her because she couldn't do it herself. I carried her to the nearby futon and called 911.

The operator asked me if she had a pulse and if she was breathing. I was too scared to check, too scared to know the answer. She wasn't cold, just lifeless. But I knew she wasn't breathing. The operator guided me through the CPR process and instructed me to wait for the paramedics. During the chest compressions a noise came from her throat like I was pushing up something stuck in her stomach. Her tongue protruded a little and probably blocked her airway. There was a big red indentation on her neck from where the rope had suffocated her. She had probably been hanging like that for some time, and the mark was palpable. It would give her problems the rest of her life hiding that mark on her neck—I still thought she would make it.

The first police officer arrived and helped me with CPR. Not long after, the paramedics came in and we rushed to the back bedroom. I thought they would help her. They let me stay in the room for a little bit, but one of them escorted me out into the living room. Several minutes later one of the paramedics came out, stood next to me and shook his head—giving me the news I wasn't prepared to accept. It didn't seem like they spent much time administering

CPR but it doesn't take long for lack of oxygen to the brain to create brain damage and she might have been past the point of any normal recovery. Within fifteen or twenty minutes of being home that night, Rachel was gone from my life forever. Her time of death was listed as 11:17 p.m.

When I received the headshake, I went to the recliner behind me and sat down. All of a sudden, feelings of guilt, shame, sadness, and confusion washed over me. I couldn't comprehend that she was able to do that to herself and I immediately wondered if there might have been someone else involved with her death.

Soon I was overcome with grief. I broke down and cried like I hadn't cried before. One of the police officers came over to me, knelt down on his knee and put his hand on my shoulder. It didn't make sense to me. She seemed better when I left. Of course my thoughts turned to our marriage issues.

It was confusing that the apartment seemed normal. There were no signs of struggle—no signs of anyone else being there. It just seemed like she came home, set her purse on the table with the bottle of wine she just purchased, and then proceeded to take her own life. How does someone take their own life like it's a routine chore—like it's something to be done at the end of the day when there's nothing else to do? How did she even know how to successfully carry it out?

The next hours of that night were extremely painful. The number of police officers at my apartment made it seem like a college fraternity had suddenly decided to use my place as a meeting spot. I wanted them to leave but they were there all night. At around 11:30 p.m. the dogs (but probably mainly Cookie) started barking while looking out the sliding glass door facing the back grassy area. I of course couldn't see anything since it was pitch black outside, and had to immediately try to quiet them down. During the rest of the night I was so ashamed that I couldn't look any of the police officers in the face and couldn't accept that they were there in my apartment during the most vulnerable moment of my life. Moreover, there was the waiting—waiting for the detective to arrive, waiting for the coroner to come and take her away, waiting for the nightmare to end. The detective arrived probably two hours later, around one in the morning. The coroner didn't arrive until close to three in the morning.

There were also the phone calls. The phone calls I had to make to her parents and my parents. The police kept asking me if I wanted someone to be with, if I wanted someone to come over. I couldn't think of anyone. It was already late and I just didn't have any close friends to call. Eventually I did call a mutual friend that had hung out with Rachel several days earlier, but it was late and she didn't come over. I ended up sitting for a long time dreading the calls I had to make. The police asked me if they could call somebody for me, but that didn't seem right. Eventually, I pressed the button on the phone to follow through with it. My parents were in shock but immediately worked on making plane reservations. Rachel's father made an incoherent noise in the background while I told her mother, who was calm and immediately in crisis mode.

I wanted to be with Rachel after the paramedics left. I wanted to hold her hand and be there for her, but the police told me I couldn't go into the room again because it was a crime scene. It wasn't until three or four in the morning when I was able to see her and say goodbye. The detective had already been in the room and they had already taken pictures of everything. The coroner had already put her on a stretcher and wrapped her in blankets. He tried to prepare her face in a way that would be pleasant but instead just looked demonic. He gave her a stupid smile and closed her eyes.

"I'm sorry," I said with tears streaming down my face. "You know I always loved you."

Days after everything happened, I of course recalled that one of Rachel's favorite Halloween costumes was Strawberry Shortcake and I remembered my conversation with the lady singer at my gig. I didn't know who that lady was and haven't spoken with her since, but I'll definitely always think of her as being some kind of conduit—a messenger from another world, a normal encounter on the surface but something more dark and cryptic underneath.

When I gave Rachel a final kiss on her cheek, chills ran down my spine. It felt like I wasn't really kissing her, more like I was kissing the illness that took her away. It was like kissing a ghost, or worse, kissing the side of her I had previously only seen in those few moments when she lost control of herself and lashed out at me in July and early August. The goodbye didn't represent all that we had been through. With suicide, there rarely are goodbyes.

Chapter 21
Pain and Intimacy

Sometimes I just feel like running away, buying a one way ticket somewhere and just starting over, fresh, away from my family. Just to do some soul searching. However, I could also just die and start over… I guess that is the perfectionist in me just wanting a clean slate and trying this thing called life all over again.

RACHEL WROTE THE journal entry above on January 4th, 2015, and I wouldn't read it until going through her Google Drive long after she passed. At the time, we were just married and living in Chicago. She hadn't found the job teaching at the university yet and was in the midst of a career change.

When I went through Rachel's things I also looked at her portfolio of poems that she had written throughout her high school and college years. They were the same poems that she first shared with me when we started dating, and I remembered sitting on her couch in the Rogers Park apartment, trying to understand the other side of her that she was showing me. It was one of our first moments being intimate by showing each other past scars.

I now noticed the dark themes that underlay some of the poems. A little-known fact told to me by her mother was that Rachel's great-grandfather was an obscure published poet named Edward Gruse. In her portfolio there were funny poems and introspective poems—she wrote an ode to the famous maraschino cherry sculpture in downtown Minneapolis, a poem about her love of lattes, and a poem about the Iraq war. The title of the portfolio was also humorous—"Use bottom cushion for flotation". But there was also a poem she wrote about a hell's angel kind of figure—a scary devil woman that no living thing can be saved from and who corrupts this wholesome world. I remembered the abuse she gave me that summer and thought of how scared I was when she transformed in front of my eyes. That was the other side of Rachel—a kind of mythic figure, like an internal deity that everyone must answer to.

In the days after Rachel's death I dealt with the reality of losing someone to suicide. I spent time trying to figure out how she actually carried out the act. I spent time going through her things and throwing items away that no longer carried any significance. Her mother gave away all her clothes, so the only item left was a pair of ankle socks that surfaced months later, hiding in one of her suitcases. I went through her wallet and pulled out the money and cards that should have been used again—I collected her music and instruments that might never be played again. I also spent time packing and moving to a new place. My parents and Rachel's family members and friends came to help me.

During that week it was hard to go outside with the dogs. How do you engage with the normal chitchat of a superficial world when you are now thrust into a world much, much below? With a numb body and mind, I went out with the dogs one day, into the woods located to the right of our apartment. The humid air was all around and normally these woods provided cool shade with dried pine needles on the ground—nothing was ever there that didn't belong to nature. That day, next to a fallen down, rotting tree to our left, were numerous plastic bags filled with something shiny and metallic. Also in the vicinity was a random watering can for flowers, though no flowers were in sight. When we inspected the bags I could tell there were a multitude of bolts and door hinges inside. The complete image of everything was abstract, as if I had stepped into the woods and was transported into a museum of contemporary art. Where did the door hinges come from and why was there a watering can there? My brain couldn't process what was on display. Further down the hill I later saw a bunch of stacked white doors, so maybe the maintenance crew ran out of space for their supplies. Strange that I had never seen anything placed in the woods like that before.

Another day, I took the dogs to the park down the hill and risked actually having to talk to someone when the prospect of small talk was almost unbearable. Some neighbor friends were there who knew what happened, and also one other person from the apartment complex who showed up with their beagle dog named Watson. I couldn't bring up my trauma with a stranger—but also couldn't be silent. Once again I was crushed inside and tried to put a mask over what felt like a gaping wound. The conversation started off normal and I wasn't sure if my neighbor friends would mention my situation—not sure if they would grant me sympathy in public. They acted like everything was normal though and I tried to play along as best I could. My wound underneath made it hard to talk as I tried to represent myself in the land of the living while I felt like I was living in the land of the dead.

"How did you name your dog?" my friend asked the owner of Watson.

"It's just from Sherlock Holmes, my boyfriend and I are big mystery fans," the girl stated with a smile.

"What are your dog's names?" she asked me.

I introduced them and gave her the typical story I had given many times before. My voice sounded far away and I was very conscious of my body language, as if I had been smoking marijuana. Hershey got so worried when he heard me talking that he made a few whining noises and left where we were standing, in the shade underneath the giant power line, and hid underneath the bench by the dog park gate—seeking refuge underneath things was what he typically did during a thunderstorm or when he felt scared. It seemed like he knew better than me that I wasn't in any shape to be fake and surfacy at a time when I was so raw. He provided my excuse that day to exit the conversation and return home.

When my folks showed up a day or so later, they greeted me at the airport with hugs and sympathy as we prepared to come to terms with my present reality. I suppose it was also their new reality in a way too, since even though they didn't cause the situation, they were somehow inadvertently part of it. We spent time together, taking the dogs out, and on one occasion my father spent part of the walk looking intently at the grass below. He was an older version of me—almost the same height, same color hair, same eye shape and same mannerisms. His eyes searched the lush, green underneath his feet and each step was methodical.

"What are you looking for?" I asked him.

"A four-leaf clover," he replied.

"I can never find those—it's too difficult," I said.

Sometime later that day he handed me one and said:

"Hopefully this will bring you better luck." I thanked him, not really sure how to respond and tucked the small leaf into my pocket.

"How did you find it?" I asked him.

"Oh, I kept searching around. I'm good at finding them."

"Really?" I said with a surprised tone of voice. I didn't think it was possible.

The clover remained in my possession for a week or so until it was tossed away like something won at a county fair, or like an old ticket stub that lost its luster. That evening we sat down for dinner at the glass table and I sat in the chair Rachel normally used for doing work on her computer. My father sat to my right, in front of the bar stools, while my mother sat directly across from me; her short, pear frame entrenched in the pleated chair. We dug in to one of the prepared meals sent to me by the community, a mishmash of pasta and vegetables.

After some minor chitchat the topic changed to expressing emotions.

"We need to be more open as a family," I said. "Rachel might've been too much at times, but she wasn't wrong in a lot of the things she told me." The comment produced a couple seconds of silence since it was not typical dinner conversation material. "She was always trying to get me to open up more and I just couldn't do it," I continued.

My father swallowed his pasta and thought for a moment. "You did what you could," he said. My mother sat with a silent expression on her face before she finally spoke:

"Greg, she was sick and not in the right state of mind." Her statement was definitive and when she finished it was supposed to be the final say on the matter.

"You don't show emotions enough," I said to her point-blank. My comment was the same one Rachel told me so many times throughout the years and it was like I was now her.

"You don't know how to treat women," my mother fired back before looking down at her plate. My father glanced at her and tried to play referee before an argument ensued. "Hey!" he said as if he was about to continue and tell us we were out of line.

My pulse was beating fast and the tension at the table had risen to well beyond normal. It seemed like her death was not only a wake-up call for me but also for our family, and I tried to express that as best I could. I soon retreated after my mother's barbed comment sunk in and the conversation slowly returned to more mundane things—even though I was representing Rachel in the matter, I was still the product of my family.

After dinner and a long day of notifying institutions of my wife's death, I lay on the futon which my parents now used; now relocated in the living room. It was the same couch I had placed Rachel's limp, lifeless body on that horrendous night.

I lay face down, exhausted after going through a traumatic day of contacting insurance companies and collecting her wedding ring from the funeral home. My parents were in chairs on either side of me, one doing a crossword puzzle and the other reading a book. As I lay there and the sky got dark, I began to feel helpless.

I wondered to myself how Rachel slipped through the cracks. Why didn't I realize she was so fragile? It just didn't seem like something she would know how to do.

My father suddenly asked, "Who was the main actor in the old Willy Wonka movie?" His head was full of trivia and he was someone you never wanted to compete against in a game of Trivial Pursuit. Even though I was practically unconscious and reeling from the day, I knew the answer to his question.

I lifted up my head. "It was Wilder," I replied in a dazed, sleepy voice.

My father repeated the question and I wondered if he had heard my answer. I became confused and frustrated. I replied with the same answer, this time, first and last name.

"It was Wilder. Alec, I mean, Gene Wilder," I said again, though not confidently. He repeated the question again. I put my head back down. Without an emotional reaction, sometimes the right answer isn't right after all. Without someone to hear, sometimes having a voice doesn't matter. I retreated back within myself.

"Oh, it was Gene Wilder," he said, as if he had come to the answer himself.

"That's what I said," I replied in an exasperated tone.

"Well, you must not have said it correctly," he said with a tone of certainty.

I put my head back down on that futon, fell asleep and dreamed—half conscious, half unconscious. My family and I used to take summer vacations in Lake Tahoe, California. Typically, we would stay at the same chalet or in the same general area of those summer rentals located just up the hill from downtown South Lake Tahoe. But one summer, we rented a house that was different from the others. As I dreamed, I was back at that house. It had an actual stream running through the middle by design. The soft, murmuring creek started outside the house, flowed through the living room, and exited beyond the white permeable wall at the room's edge. I was at ease, like in a serene, peaceful dream as I slept there at night. The water flowed in a constant small, steady stream—the complete opposite of the overflowing creek that had flooded near our Virginia apartment that rainy June. The reassuring flow was also different than the wild rapids of the excursion Rachel and I had taken on the Middle Fork Flathead River in Montana.

One morning during that childhood summer, I awoke to the simultaneous sounds of the water rushing through the room and Enya coming from my CD player, which I had programmed the night before. Her New Age Celtic style with eerie melodies and drone-like synthesizers was the most relaxing, soothing music I had ever heard. As I lay there listening to Enya's calming voice, I thought about my family sleeping in the other rooms—my grandparents, my uncle, my parents, and my sister. There was a feeling of completeness—that everything was happening as it should and everyone was at the right place at the right time. All of my anxieties were gone. Anything that gave me pain had subsided and any fear I had was lifted.

I also went back further in time. I started to dream more deeply. Years before the family trip to Lake Tahoe, around the age of six or seven, I had encountered the dark side of my own personality. I lived in a bright yellow house on the corner of Metaline Street in a medium-sized town in eastern Washington. It was a plain, cozy house that had a great yard for playing games like Kick-the-Can, or for wrestling with other neighborhood kids. Across the street and over to the right lived some of my close friends. Initially, my best childhood friend had lived in that light blueish house, which had a great side yard for throwing the football and playing sports. There was also a short, gray brick wall in the side yard that was crumbling in some places. You could take the bricks apart if you could lift them, and they gave the yard a malleable quality, easily influenced by its residents.

When that friend moved away to Pasadena, a Mormon family moved in and I became friends with two of the boys (more so with the older brother closer to my age). I think the family had four kids total, with one on the way. In the backyard of that blue house was a trampoline. The two boys were fairly athletic, able to do all kinds of tricks and jumps, and I enjoyed going over to their house to jump with them and have carefree fun. One day while jumping on their trampoline I came down funny or accidentally "bounced" the younger brother. When I "bounced" him, he went flying off the trampoline and landed hard on the grass below. It was nothing serious as far as child's play goes, but he was nonetheless upset.

My reaction to this normal childhood accident was shock, guilt, and horror. It wasn't the first time I brought pain to a friend—I once accidentally kneed my other childhood friend in the balls while we were playing football and he was laid out on the couch writhing in pain for the rest of the day. Based on this and other similar moments in my childhood, it was like I had somehow caused the trampoline injury and although it wasn't on purpose, it felt like I was destined to hurt my friends or people that were close to me. I ran home and hid underneath my bed—not a typical response for a seven year-old child.

Steve (the older brother), Phillip (the younger one who was hurt), and a couple other kids came over to my house looking for me.

From my hiding spot, I could hear the gang knock on the door to my house.

"Is Greg here?" Steve asked my Mom.

"I don't know, I didn't hear him come home," she said.

"Well we think he's here because he left our house upset and ran this way."

"You're welcome to look in his room. He might be in there," she replied.

The reason I was hiding under the bed was that I knew they would come looking for me—and because I couldn't deal with what I was feeling.

After entering my room, the gang discovered my hiding spot. Steve peeked underneath the bed:

"Greg, what are you doing?" he said with a smile.

"I'm hiding."

"Come out so we can keep playing. Phil is fine."

"No, I don't wanna. I'll just hurt somebody else."

"Ah, come on. It was an accident. Phil isn't mad at ya."

Phillip was a good-natured kid. He was going to be more cautious around me, but assuredly not angry.

"Come on! Come out and play," they all chimed in.

Did the peer pressure work? I think my self-pity kept me at home for at least a little while longer and I eventually reconvened with the gang later that day.

The feeling that arose most from that incident came from directly or indirectly causing pain to someone close to me. Was it something I subconsciously did on purpose? If so, how does that happen? Did I initiate pain, and then recoil in guilt and shame? If so, where did the shame come from? These were all things I couldn't comprehend as a child, and so I hid underneath my bed. Even if I'd had a bad reaction to a normal childhood accident, I felt like I had touched upon something deeper and darker.

I also remembered the time some of my best friends moved away. My reaction was extreme—I brooded in my bedroom for hours. Sometimes I would cry myself to sleep. I don't remember why I reacted the way I did, but I became familiar with the suffering. It became a feeling I almost grew to miss at times because instead of receiving the comfort, compassion and healing that I needed from my home environment, I turned to the pain as something I could rely on. It reminded me of one of my father's favorite stories—of how as an infant alone in my bedroom I deliberately hit my head on the floor in order to create a scene, wherein my mother would come rushing in. Who knew that pain and intimacy could be joined together like they were somehow related?

When I came to that night, it was time to go to my own bedroom. It was late and quiet, like when a clock stops ticking. I had gone back in time to a place it seemed I would never return. I remembered a lot of childhood memories the year after she died—the layers carefully placed one on top of the other were stripped away. I wondered which memory was more important and why they came up. I slowly crawled into bed and waited for the next day.

Chapter 22
Shiva

It is not society that is to guide and save the creative hero, but precisely the reverse. And so every one of us shares the supreme ordeal—carries the cross of the redeemer—not in the bright moments of his tribe's great victories, but in the silence of his personal despair.

—Joseph Campbell, Writer & Philosopher

THE MEMORIAL SERVICE took place in Plymouth, Minnesota at the end of August. I wore the same pink-colored tie from our wedding day, a black sash given to me as part of the shiva, and some white sunglasses because those were all that I owned. I didn't have to wear the sunglasses, but the shame that I felt made me want to disappear amongst my in-law's many family and friends in attendance. The day was warm and sunny, with green grass and the smell of summer all around. A line of many cars appeared out of nowhere, and soon the whole cemetery was full of people paying their respects. Next to the casket about to be lowered in the ground was a white tent with rows of chairs underneath. Her parents sat in the front row with myself to the right and after the rabbi gave his speech, they lowered the wooden box into the large hole in front of us. I placed my hand on her father's knee as the mechanical contraption slowly clinked and clanked with the brown box descending in front of us. My hand was there for support, though I was also afraid. It was like being at the top of a roller coaster about to drop into the depths below, and we had front row seats to experience the ensuing grief to its fullest. When it was all over, the two families huddled together in two different sides—my family and I stood silent next to a tree to the right of the burial site, while her family huddled together closer to the filled-in hole. All of the people paying their respects lined up to console Rachel's grieving family. Nobody visited us and we were left with an isolated, prismatic view of a community in mourning. Again I felt shame, as if I was responsible for the situation now unfolding.

Days later I returned to her gravesite with friends, and we each took turns being eaten by mosquitos and trying to say something memorable about her. A month earlier I was talking to her face-to-face. Now I was looking at her while staring into the ground, a stark reminder of where we all end up someday.

"I just couldn't let her go," I said out loud. The reality was that she was the one who let go and I thought about the common phrase, "If you really love someone, let them go." Maybe in her desperation she tried to provide some kind of grace or perverse act of love.

I returned to Charlottesville in a dazed state. I had time off from my new job and didn't go back to work until October. Since it's a bureaucratic institution, law enforcement and their investigations are not by nature equipped to deal with people who have undergone traumatic loss and grief. In the case of Rachel, the biggest question I had at the time was if there was foul play or someone else involved. I can obviously look back and say that most likely she did it to herself. But I didn't know for sure at the time and I didn't see how she could carry out such an act. I also didn't understand the timeline of events leading up to her death and I wanted some kind of clarity.

Bureaucratic institutions with lots of procedures and protocols move very slowly. It wasn't until September that I had a decent conversation with the detective about her death. I told him about questions I had regarding the crime scene and about a couple things that didn't add up.

"Your wife wrote something down in a diary that night," he told me.

"She didn't have a diary," I responded.

"Well, there was a journal we found and it had some stuff she had been writing."

"It was normal for her to write things down in a note from time to time. She sometimes left notes by places I might be so I could read about her thoughts or feelings," I said, trying to explain that it was normal behavior.

"Well, she wrote some things in a journal that night," the detective told me. There was a brief pause.

"I have some questions about the placement of the stepladder," I said, changing the topic since it didn't seem like he was going to say much more about what she wrote. "It seemed like the ladder was placed in the opposite direction. Like, if she used it to set everything up, fine, but if she used it to eventually kill herself, the ladder should have been placed the other way. Her body was facing the opposite direction of the ladder."

"Hmm, I'm not sure about that. Mr. Duncan, with all due respect, I think your wife intended to do what she did."

"Did you find any receipt in the bag with the bottle of wine?"

"No, there was no receipt."

"Well, there was a charge on her debit card from that day. If I forward that information to you, could you find out when and where she got that bottle? I think it would help with the timeline of when things happened."

"Sure, I'll look into that for you."

That was the extent of our conversation that afternoon in September, and I assumed he was referring to what Rachel already told me about when I saw her writing something that day. Many times that fall my anxiety would get the best of me, and I would lay in bed afraid of someone or something taking my life like what happened to Rachel. I truly believed there was a possibility she was murdered and as I look back now, I realize that she *was* murdered—by the dissociated side of her own self. She was murdered by her unknown face.

The police knew of course that it was suicide, just never made that clear. That was why they would be so casual with the rest of the investigation. When there's little communication from the authorities, people get desperate. It was the same reason I actually hired a private detective at one point to follow up a lead about where she got the mysterious bottle of wine from—a 1.5 liter bottle of a cabernet sauvignon merlot blend by Frontera, made in Chile, that I had never seen her purchase before. After the original detective determined it must've been paid for in cash (no electronic record), I initially assumed it was probably from a nearby convenience store and used the private detective to get security footage, since the original detective never informed me that he already looked into it. I first went there myself towards the end of August, but the clerk told me the manager wasn't there and couldn't help me. I went back around September 4ᵗʰ with a friend and a preservation of evidence letter informing them of the police investigation. When a week went by and it seemed like the detective wasn't following up, I paid the private detective to try and help bring some kind of closure and keep my mind from spinning. He contacted them on September 12th and relayed his findings to me. Apparently, the surveillance video at the store ran on a four-day loop and by the time it was investigated, too much time had passed. I later learned that the bottle could've been bought at any store really, and I just went to the closest, logical location to where we lived. Why did I have to hire a private detective to find all that out?

Chapter 23
Communication from Another Source

Oh, what if one could only see
That through Faith, we can be free
Free from hate, and agony

Souls from above have told us,
Souls who protect and hold us
Souls know The World, so reverently.

Love circumvents disaster,
Love is indeed THE MASTER,
Love for all life, and for all whom we see.

Ancients of Ages past agree
We'll fulfill our Destiny
If Our Hearts Could Only See

—Billy Harper, Saxophonist

WHEN A TRAUMATIC moment happens in someone's life, time has a tendency to stop. I soon went to support groups and noticed how people counted the days, and even hours since their loved one passed away. The moment seemed forever etched in their psyche and it was very easy to keep living in the past, like living in a different dimension—being suspended in a realm where night comes before night, where there's day without day; time is eternal, time is forgotten.

The most influential song after Rachel's death was without a doubt saxophonist Billy Harper's "If Our Hearts Could Only See." The song was on a recording by trumpet player Eddie Henderson, and it was one of the featured ballads. Every time I drove my car that fall, the song would be in my mix and, time after time, my ears pricked up. It wasn't your typical jazz ballad either, the melody was spiritual, almost hymn-like, with dark undertones. There was something in the song's melody and message that stuck with me and I started listening to it more and more until I found the original recording by Harper. The song gave me comfort and solace when I needed it the most, and I used to listen to it repeatedly before going to bed. It was like Rachel played a part in finding the song, because I always felt she was there trying to help comfort me at a time when the feeling of tremendous loss covered me like a heavy blanket. Even though I stumbled across the song myself, it was as if there was something else leading me to that song and trying to reassure me.

When Rachel's Charlottesville memorial service took place at the beginning of September, the Billy Harper song was one of its focal points. It was featured on the program and I put a band together to perform the song. There were a lot of other great musical tributes that day from friends and colleagues because Rachel knew and worked with so many talented musicians, but I remember my song the most. Not only is the melody of the song beautiful and spiritual, but it also has lyrics that were especially appropriate for the situation. Harper stated in an interview with Suzan and Willard Jenkins that the melody of the song came to him in a dream when some entity from above reached down and handed him a cassette tape. He played the tape, heard the beautiful melody, and transcribed it after awakening from the dream. When I personally asked him about this later after one of his concerts, he said that while he was known for hearing melodies in dreams and immediately writing them down, he came up with this particular song at the piano during a solemn mood. When I asked him, he was a lot older than during the previous interview so maybe his memory was fuzzy.

Rachel appeared in messages and it forced me again to the realm of magical thinking—a realm I hadn't really visited since the pseudo-schizophrenic time in grad school. When I went to the first support group meeting, a whiteboard hanging on the wall caught my eye. The meetings took place at a local church, in a room used for Sunday school classes and other community functions. The somber mood never really lifted after everyone shared their grief story and offered what sympathy they could. To the left of my place at the long table, a rectangular whiteboard faced me, not too far from the solitary window. Although some of the writing had been erased and some of the sentences were not complete, I could clearly make out a message that read:

"Thanks…Sorry…Please be happy."

There would be conversations later on where I could hear or feel what Rachel would say in that moment. While visiting a winery with my sister and her family, the discussion turned to abolishing the Electoral College and the pros and cons of playing the trumpet—I automatically could sense Rachel lighting up and becoming a passionate participant in the conversation. I almost knew the things she might have said. Again, she wasn't there, but it seemed like she almost was. On one occasion, I was walking the dogs with some of my friend's children and they were very interested in Cookie and Hershey, and asked me many questions about them. Rachel was there as well—there because I could almost hear the things she would have said to the kids—there, because she normally was.

There were times things would go missing and I couldn't understand how. There was the missing soap from the shower, the missing hot chocolate packet, and the missing CD, left behind after Cookie chewed its case. The worst scenario was at school when I set my computer down for one minute and it disappeared for about a month. I thought I was going crazy when the computer didn't re-appear, but apparently, a fellow teacher had walked off with it on their cart and somehow didn't realize they had it.

There was the time I came back home and the clock was on a completely different time even though the battery was fine, and the time a glass baking dish (made for the oven) shattered into pieces while cooking. I woke up once at 1:30 a.m. to a two-second loud beep, but didn't know what it would have come from, or if it really happened. There were walks in the nearby woods with the dogs, where two bored teenagers carried around a laptop that produced very realistic and disturbing female screaming sounds. When I practiced my trumpet, I would every now and again have the sensation that someone was flicking my hair. At first, I didn't think anything of it—later on it became annoying and I would stop practicing and have to touch my hair to make sure I wasn't crazy. I acknowledged her presence in my mind, though I didn't quite know how to react to it. If you believe in ghosts, then you're supposed to understand that most of what they do is for the purpose of being acknowledged or recognized, but what's the proper way to do that?

There was also the time I was driving to a meeting around 5 p.m. and saw someone that looked like Rachel pass me in a white Bronco. As I approached the car, I could have looked over at the woman to make sure, but I was too freaked out—too embarrassed to stare at a complete stranger. That was the only time since her death I've seen someone who looked like her.

Most of the time I didn't talk about my personal life with colleagues. They didn't ask either because it just wasn't professional. However, one day after school I chatted with two fellow teachers in the hall. One of them had asked me a leading question and it opened the door for me to share my pain and struggles.

"The things I have learned the past months about Rachel are things that would have taken me a year or two to learn if she was still alive," I said, realizing the tragedy of my statement. "Events happen, and they force you to think and take a hard look at yourself," I continued.

As I walked home that day, an isolated storm was brewing. There was intermittent rain and the wind started to blow like there was a mini typhoon. Due to all the trees in my neighborhood and in Virginia in general, it's common for the wind to break off some of the dried-out branches. On that day, as I stepped into my yard with a multitude of tall trees, a big branch broke off and landed about ten or twenty feet in front of me. The branch shot straight into the ground like a vertical toothpick, seemingly becoming another tree. My dumbfoundedness made me do a double-take to make sure the branch was the same one that broke off. If I had been about fifteen feet ahead of myself, the branch probably would have killed or seriously injured me. My interpretation in the moment was that Rachel didn't appreciate my slowness in understanding her and somehow vented her anger through the fallen branch.

One time I was playing the piano in the music room on a cold night around 10 p.m. The headphones covered my ears, since it was late and past the time of producing audible noise. I finished playing, took off my headphones, and right at that moment I distinctly heard someone say, "I'm at your door" or "I'm at your front door." I looked outside, looked around but couldn't see anybody. I couldn't tell initially where it came from because the music room had a separate outside entrance located through an adjacent sunroom. The entire area was visible from the outside because of all the glass. Since no one was visible, perhaps someone was at my front door, located on the other side of the house. There was no one, however. At the time, I assumed it was someone next door at the neighbors. It didn't entirely make sense though since it was late, and normally there wouldn't be visitors at that time. It reminded me of how Rachel's mother said that the doorbell on the back door of their house would ring indiscriminately. Perhaps Rachel was at some kind of spiritual door and trying to get through. Or maybe I was still trying to hold onto someone who was supposed to be a part of my life forever.

After everything happened that summer, I wrote down notes in my phone. I had an overwhelming need to record what happened because I was dealing with things that couldn't be explained—things that bordered on paranormal. Seemingly normal occurrences took on greater significance under the weight of trauma, and my senses were locked into anything and everything out of the ordinary.

One such event that sticks out above all others is what happened at my restaurant gig that evening with the singer. There were other surreal moments in the months that followed—things that could be explained in a rational way, but under the circumstances left me questioning. One such instance involved the time I sent Rachel flowers in July. She was working at the music festival in Los Angeles and this was the point when she was dealing with the girl in the email. On September 28th, more than a month after her death, a flower package of my own arrived at my doorstep. By that time I had moved out of the apartment and into a different rental house hidden in woods off the beaten path. The package was similar to what I sent Rachel. It included a box of chocolates, some flowers (not roses though), and a broken vase. If I were to explain this rationally, it was simply a case of someone sending flowers to the previous tenant of the house and not having their new address. Silk pillowcases also showed up at my door, and they later found their way to my driveway, picked up by a merciful junk removal service. I thought of Rachel each time though, and felt a connection I could hold onto.

On October 12th, a nose ring/stud that was similar to the kind Rachel would frequently lose appeared out of nowhere in the bathroom. The stud was a pin that had a perpendicular end hook and included a single small diamond or faux diamond at the end. It was placed on a small dish we often kept near the sink on the counter, and I didn't think it was hers since the coroner already gave me the one she had on when she died. It seemed strange that such a random object would materialize in such a manner and it again gave me a connection back to Rachel that I could hold onto—I wanted to believe she was still somehow around.

During one of the walks with the dogs, we walked to the end of the path by a large river and saw a woman sitting absolutely still on a large rock. It was a walk we had done many times before and we would occasionally see people, but rarely someone sitting at this particular spot. She had dark hair and as we slowly approached her, we waited a little to see if she would move—to see some other part of her face or head. Her body was like a statue though and her head didn't waver. The front facade was a mystery—something left to the imagination. The lady clearly didn't want anyone to see that side. We turned around and headed back with the Athena condo units in front of us to the right, the river to the left. All of the sudden, the word "Cookie!" became audible in my ear. I turned around, but could no longer see the lady. I didn't know where the sound came from and started to doubt whether I heard it at all. When we went back towards the car, we diverted our path and spent some time in the nearby field. Before heading over the bridge, we saw the same lady again, now sitting on a metallic bench. Her back was towards us and once more, she never moved—like breathing was not part of her body's vocabulary.

There were other moments too of course. There were the empty seats next to me when I traveled or when I was at a restaurant with family. The first time I noticed the empty space was when I was in therapy and the two different therapists always placed a vacant seat next to them during the session. Perhaps it was some kind of trick psychiatrists use, but it definitely made me think Rachel was in the other chair, listening, going through the therapy sessions with me. If I thought about it, I would become sad so I tried not to think about it that much. It was uncanny though, how often there were empty seats next to me—empty seats at bars, on planes, and at events. At one point, there was an extra ticket for a private party. Since I couldn't get anyone else to join me, I went to the party by myself; and after going in the entrance to get my hand stamped, there I was holding the extra ticket, the ticket that Rachel would have used if she were still alive. It sounds strange, but I assumed Rachel didn't want anyone else to go with me, so somehow I went with her.

In November, an unusual gig request to perform showed up in my email. It's not uncommon for musicians to receive strange requests and if you're in the business long enough, you accumulate stories. Case in point, I once played an Indian wedding at the Cultural Center in downtown Chicago, where I marched around the building following the bride and groom. While the bride paraded around on a white horse, the other trumpet player and I kept repeating the same song because that was the only one we knew that sounded good under the circumstances. The request from November started as follows:

> *Hello, I want to plan a mini show for my boyfriend. I also want trumpeter to give insight/tips about improving as a trumpeter in general, and how to jumpstart a career. It is very important that my boyfriend knows how to connect and communicate with other musicians.*

Rachel always pushed me to become better at networking and she was exasperated seeing me flounder when I should have flourished. Even though the request came from Matteson, Illinois (where I coincidentally first started teaching trumpet lessons) and was from someone I never met, the request could have very well been something she made. She wanted me to communicate better and advocate for myself and so it seemed like I was reading a message from her. By that time, I was of course living in Virginia, so I just referred someone else for the job. But once again, there was a connection to Rachel that I could hold onto when holding onto something was what I desperately needed.

Rachel came to me in other songs too. While going to Blue Mountain Brewery in Virginia with some mutual friends, the song "All I Have To Do Is Dream" by the Everly Brothers came on the speaker outside and it made me think of her since, dreaming was my only way to reach her now. There was also the time I was sitting on the couch listening to a Terence Blanchard record from the '80s. While I listened, a picture on Facebook of Rachel and I dancing at a wedding we attended the previous year appeared. Immediately after seeing the picture, Donald Harrison (the saxophone player) came in with the band's rendition of "Somewhere" by Leonard Bernstein. I lost it—overwhelmed by the emotion of the moment and the sense of loss. It was the same song I practiced over and over again on the piano as a way to express my grief. A poet once said that "death is the absence that is forever present." I was feeling that absence and it was something easier to connect with in a song.

I don't think I would have later remembered any of those events after she passed—all of those casual, surreal moments from my life. But I recorded them all, all of the odd occurrences. They connected me to her the more she faded away.

Chapter 24
Dreams

Dreams are important to the soul—not for the messages the ego takes from them, not for the recovered memories or the revelations; what does seem to matter to the soul is the nightly encounter with a plurality of shades in an underworld, as if dreams prepared for death, the freeing of the soul from its identity with the ego and the waking state.

—James Hillman

ONE EVENING IN the first year after her death, I sat on the couch watching TV with the dogs. I was now renting a new house in Charlottesville, located on the other side of town, off of Hydraulic road in a neighborhood tucked away in a small wooded area. A news program came on and the reporter stated: *"A clash of extremes occurred August 12th, 2017. Neo-Nazi, far right, white supremacy groups battled with counter-protesters, including the far-left anti-Fascist group Antifa. The riot that followed rocked the city as well as the nation, since it marked a new era in extreme political polar opposites."*

The voice carried on but I no longer paid attention. I remembered that day and began to doze off. The reporter continued: *"Fear from both sides forced them to the extremes."* Suddenly, Cookie barked and woke me up. The program was now on commercial, but I started to wonder. Perhaps the fear was that they had more in common than they knew. Perhaps the fear was that they were stronger together than apart. Perhaps they had a fear that if they met in the middle, they would expose their true identities. Each side resorted to putting on a mask and letting a false self deal with the issues at hand. Maybe the ensuing pain and struggle was a way to break free from that shell and connect when nothing else seemed possible—like a lab experiment where a union of unlike substances creates a chemical reaction, trying to fabricate something new.

I dozed off again with the monotone news reporter voice in the background. The wind blew violently outside and rain hit the window intermittently, creating a sound like a broken typewriter. In a half-awake, half-asleep state, I had a dream of sorts. Rachel's face peered down at us from outside, seeing where we were. She had exaggerated features—a long pointy nose turned to the side as her large eyes peered sideways from above the backyard window. Her face was white and ghostly, like a head without a body. I could tell she wanted inside but couldn't enter. Both the dogs and I were hiding on the couch as I tried to evade her look, afraid of what might happen next.

I next dreamed about myself and Rachel putting on masks. My new false self forced me to hide in the woods where Rachel couldn't find me. I went there out of fear, afraid she would see me. While in the woods, abundant with vegetation, I seemed to be running in the opposite direction I wanted to go. I eventually stumbled across an opening where I could peer back and see where Rachel was. Her new false self enlisted a few people around her to help with a large rock she carried. I could see that she was also afraid, fearful that those who helped would see something in the rock. When nothing seemed to work, she set the rock down and started to weep. I woke up in a dazed state and thought to myself: Fear forced us to the extremes. It kept us from what was at the core of each other and our marriage.

The TV program in the background still continued:

"Charlottesville had to wrestle with the fact that maybe it wasn't as good of a place as it thought it was. The response

was that the riot didn't truly reflect the essence of the community. Even so, one was left wondering—what was the city's true identity and who really represented it?

Rachel came to me in other dreams. The first dream was on September 4th and she said she would come back since I missed her. A month or so later I dreamed I met Rachel somewhere and when she saw me, she ran away and threw herself into a car and was run over. It was terrifying and devastating at the same time. Eventually, in other dreams, Rachel and I were together again and spending time with one another. She had made some random friends and we were hanging out with them as well, or they were around. But every time I tried to talk about our relationship or her issues, she went away.

We set up dates in other dreams—one that was supposed to be at a place next to O'Hare airport in Chicago but the dream ended before the rendezvous. Another date ended with me holding her and telling her I didn't want her to leave. One of the most beautiful and emotional dreams was the time I felt like she was there next to the bed saying goodbye to me. It was early in the morning before I had to teach at school and it was the same way she used to say goodbye to me when she had someplace to go to early and I was still in bed. She would be quiet and speak so tenderly. Her presence was peaceful and loving. It was the goodbye I never got from her in real life. I woke up that morning with tears in my eyes. I couldn't believe I remembered what it was like when she would say goodbye to me like that. It was one of those memories of her that had almost faded away. I cried and tried to enjoy the moment, even though it was painful.

In later dreams, Rachel and I were kissing and making up when I asked her where she went (I guess I was referring to where she disappeared to after she passed). She said she first went to Sacramento, then Mexico. I asked how she got through the border with her passport if it said she was dead. In a later dream, Rachel was working out on a rowing machine. She told me she was going to Japan.

She said I could go with her if I wanted. I thought about when she died and the thought of the empty rowing machine was too much. I sobbed.

The most interesting dream occurred between the previous two, when I dreamed I was in a hotel room. After a while I realized Rachel was in a room adjacent to mine passed out, possibly from drinking. I immediately became worried that she might harm herself so I went to her room. The door had a digital keypad lock that indicated there were three messages (perhaps from Rachel). I went through the door easily without reading the messages. I saw the bed where she had been sleeping and saw the imprint of her body in the covers. I went over to the bathroom and saw her sleeping on the floor. She woke up, lifted up her head, and said: "I'm leaving me."

Another dream I had around the same time sticks out because of its enigmatic nature. In the dream, I was with a short girl with short hair. I pulled a tent-like canopy or large parachute over the top of us so that we were covered underneath. It used to be a game I played as a kid during PE where all the children would run underneath a big parachute and suddenly be inside a giant protected dome. After safely being covered from above, I held the girl and tried to kiss her. But just at that moment, she excused herself and said there was something she needed to get first. She came back wearing a blue ornate mask. The mask had two small points that came out from the top and featured several reflective pieces of jewelry or coloring on the sides. I was surprised and a little put off. I took the mask off and told her it wasn't necessary. She now looked a little different than before, but I still proceeded to embrace and kiss her. The girl suddenly said to me:

"That's the point."

Of course, the dogs didn't have much better dreams. Hershey and Cookie were there when Rachel died. I asked them to tell me what happened. I begged them and pleaded with them to tell me. I knew they couldn't of course, but in some way, I think they tried. Cookie became a lot more vocal after that night, as if she was trying to tell me about it.

Both dogs would occasionally cry in their sleep for the next five months. There would be moments in the middle of the night when I would be sleeping and I would hear a howl. One night in early January, Hershey's cry sounded like he was saying "Noooooooo." I immediately went to comfort him. Sometimes they would just howl without being asleep.

In October, Rachel's parents visited from out of town and stopped by the house. When Hershey saw Rachel's mother, he immediately went up to her and seemed to tell her everything he had been holding in, with a kind of whining noise I'd never heard him make before. In fact, I haven't heard him sound like that before or since. It sounded as if he was talking to her and telling her about what happened and how he was sorry and that he was so scared. If I was more of an emotional person, I would have done the same thing.

On February 14th, I dreamed that I was at some kind of support group when a lady with a golden retriever asked me a question I didn't understand. Another guy replied that with suicide there's a tear in the fabric of someone's life and it creates a gaping wound that can't heal. One viable option to close the gap is to die. Nearly at the same time as he said this, a car went over a cliff. I thought the car was permanently damaged but it had some skis on the bottom and it was able to go off a cliff and continue fine on the road below. The car did this maneuver several times.

On March 19th, I had a dream where people were murdering each other. They threw their own parents onto a fire and stabbed them to death. Sometime later that spring, I had a vivid dream about some creatures living in a hole in the ground underneath the side of a house. I could only see their bright shiny eyes. I threw them some bark to see if they would come out, but they didn't so I couldn't see what they were. I was too scared to go into their hole and confront them. Many months later I dreamed about a demon figure jumping around and attacking and biting people. I observed this like a movie. Green stuff would come up when the demon bit into someone.

Those were the most disturbing dreams. I also had humorous or absurd ones about the future. I once dreamed that airplane attendants were replaced by floating trays and that Oprah Winfrey died exercising on her Peloton bike. In January I dreamed I was a detective and had to find a missing person who resembled the actor Michael Nearpass. Since I have a shark phobia, one of the scarier dreams was when I was water skiing with a friend who looked like Jamie Lee Curtis. A big great white shark came toward her and I didn't know how to help her. Fortunately, it didn't do anything, and I could see the big gray shark swim underneath us.

Rachel had a common dream of her own that she told me once. She termed it a "stress dream" because it was full of anxiety with no particular cause. This is the dream in her own words:

> At a crazy weird yoga class in NYC with all my stuff. My family was there too but let me go to the class alone. I changed my clothes for the class so I had to take stuff out of my suitcase—so when the class was over, I had to put the stuff back in my suitcase. I couldn't fit it in there and there seemed to be endless amounts of clothes, books, and music. I tried to fit it all in and it took me an hour at least; and then my family came to get me and I still was trying to get my stuff in the suitcase. It didn't seem like a dream at all.

In real life, whenever there was too much "stuff" for her to process, she would give up and hand it over to someone else, like a partner or family member. When she couldn't overcome all she was dealing with that summer, she gave up her life and left her issues for others to sort through.

Chapter 25
The Police

The curing of rage is an arduous journey since it consists in relinquishing illusions, accepting the teachings of anger, asking help from the instinctive psyche and helping the dead find peace.
—Clarissa Pinkola Estés, Writer & Psychologist

BY THE END of January, the police detective finally met with me and released a photocopy of the note she wrote and left behind. Those six months after her death were agonizing because of my brain's constant spinning, trying to think about all the details. I kept on thinking there was something missing and maybe someone else was involved. Eventually, I got tired and the spinning slowly lost momentum. At some point I couldn't think any more about it because my brain felt so heavy and weighed down. As winter came, hope meant any kind of news—anything that would shed light on what happened.

We met at the police headquarters at the end of January in a small conference room near the front desk. The police detective, whom I first met briefly that night in August and spoke with on the phone in September, now had a beard. It was neither trim nor bushy, but somewhere in between. In remembering his appearance between the months of August and January I sometimes confused his face with the lead paramedic's face, the one that gave me the indication Rachel didn't make it—an angular face with a pointy chin and soulless eyes. This face now sitting across from me was different, slightly rounder and covered with a dark beard. He didn't look like the same person I remembered, but his matter-of-fact tone was similar. His voice seemed to hide insecurity, or hint that he had gone into the profession with a greater deal of sympathy than he now possessed.

When we sat down, he stated: "To be honest Mr. Duncan, I'm meeting with you out of professional courtesy. Some of my colleagues wondered why I'm even meeting when it's not required of me and quite frankly, I don't have to take the time to set up this meeting. You could've just come in to pick up this packet and been on your way. But I know you have questions, and so I wanted to be here to help answer any questions you had about the investigation."

I didn't read the photocopied note he handed me until I got home that evening. Instead, I talked with the detective, asked my questions, and tried to explain how his lack of communication during the previous months made this process even worse. He sat across from me at a large round table.

"Mr. Duncan, there are parts of my job I wish could be different. For example, when someone dies it's difficult to separate family and friends from that deceased individual, but it's a crime scene and has to be treated that way. I don't enjoy doing that."

When he made this statement, tears came to my eyes. The memory of waiting outside the back bedroom for hours while Rachel was inside was too much.

There were two times that winter when I became so frustrated that I got angry and lost control. This time the anger was different than when Rachel would repeatedly push my buttons. Instead of being a knee-jerk response to provocation, this anger was built up over time—a result of dealing with systems outside of my control. The frustration from dealing with bureaucracy was tapping into emotions and feelings about myself that I had buried. It felt like being kicked while I was still down, and all the self-value I had seemed to be erased. Was I really just a selfish jerk? Why am I a failure in life?

When I came home from the meeting with the detective at the end of January, I read the note Rachel had written. I had started to make dinner prior to reading it and there was a knife lying on the kitchen counter.

He keeps trying to tell me that I don't like him and that I don't love him but if I didn't this wouldn't be so hard. I did love him. I wanted to tell him all the time and it hurts for him to tell me that I never did. He is so unemotional when he says it too. I was so happy when we got married and I don't understand how he could say these things. He's making me feel so bad and it hurts beyond belief. I can't stay with him when he constantly makes me feel this way but it is so hard to leave because I know most of his problems (are) because of his upbringing. Underneath it all there could be this wonderful person but he is so concerned with protecting his fragile ego that he can't even understand my feelings or validate them....

I always love people that can't love me back...why? I don't know how to break this pattern. Maybe I should just end my life since I'm always going to be disappointed by love. I don't see a reason to live at this point. I don't have someone who sees me, hears me, and loves me. I don't know why this always happens to me. This feeling is so draining and I'm not sure I want to live with this feeling anymore. I just want to be truly loved and for some reason I can't be. I have no life purpose so why bother. I give up....

I drank because nobody heard me and nobody cared, except my parents did care. Greg will probably want to say all this is because of alcohol, but not feeling loved by a partner for 7 years (with infidelity) would probably cause anyone to want to escape these thoughts and drink.

As soon as I finished reading the last part, I took the knife and threw it across the room. It hit the wall with a sharp clank and landed with a thud. So that's it? There was nothing else between us? Seven years and nothing? I went across the room to pick up the knife and inspected the now-damaged object. The tip was curled up enough that I couldn't bend it back into place and it would prove difficult to fit the blade back into the knife rack. It could be used again, just not in any normal way.

Earlier that winter, I read an email the police detective sent me. I had inquired about the confiscated computers and devices and when I was going to get them back. In his response, he said:

Unfortunately, in certain cases, especially those involving a death, certain items must remain with the police department. Regardless of who they belonged to initially, they become evidence which must be retained...I will check on the availability of the other items (computers and devices) but some of those may not be returned to you either.

I was practicing in the music room when I read the email. My blood started to boil—it seemed like the system was mocking me. All I wanted was some sense of normalcy, some type of closure. I picked up the music stand and threw it into the ground. I lifted it back up and slammed it down again.

"What the fuck!? Goddammit! The investigation is over. Why are they keeping my fucking computer?" I blurted out.

The answer was that they didn't need the devices and the detective was just spitting out bureaucratic bullshit. They eventually returned my property, so I finally became relieved. But the anger and consternation exposed something I hadn't yet realized. I was angry at myself. Why do bad things happen to me and to people around me, I wondered. The anger and hurt ran pretty deep, deeper than I could comprehend. Rachel used to feel powerless after life dealt her rejection or disappointment. That was now me, and receiving that humiliation first brings shame. Anger soon follows.

Chapter 26
The Cave

In my symptom is my soul.

—James Hillman

SOMETIME DURING THE winter after her death, I watched a documentary about an amazing archaeological discovery in the Yucatán Peninsula. The crux was that they discovered some well-preserved bones in one of the famous cenotes (underground caves filled with water) of Mexico. Some of those bones were human. The documentary explained how the bones of a prehistoric teenage girl ended up at the bottom of this watery cave.

The girl wandered into the dark cave, most likely seeking shelter, food, or water. At that time in history, the cave was not inundated but did have small sources of water. As she entered further, daylight faded. Lush vegetation changed to strange rock formations. She used a torch to find her way and eventually that torch went out. The girl wandered further down the cave until she reached a point where she became lost. I wondered if this was similar to how Rachel felt that summer, that perhaps she was wandering through the dark part of her soul. Next, the girl stumbled onto a huge drop-off hidden in the dark. She couldn't see it and fell a hundred feet to her death in the cavern below—a kind of black hole that swallowed her up. When the cave filled up with water throughout the years, it preserved her bones for future archaeologists to discover. The tragedy in the case of the prehistoric girl was that she only tried to protect herself. How was she supposed to know the cave was dangerous? How could she know there was no return?

Initially I was the calm within the storm for Rachel. I imagined that Rachel was like the girl in the documentary and that I was like the fire in the torch that she held onto while going deeper in the cave. We both somehow led each other to that place. She knew I wasn't emotional enough for her or able to validate her emotions when she really needed me to. But I was steady, always there, never getting too high or too low. She saw that as something she could hold onto when her own life was too much. We had a common bond, a common understanding that ran deep—we were both in that cave together. Our love for each other was evident, just buried beneath our own issues. Gradually over time, Rachel needed more from me. By the time my own issues crept up on me, the light went out and Rachel was left in the dark without a way out. Perhaps we were led astray by each other, perhaps by something else. While she didn't make it out alive, I sometimes feel like I'm still in that cave and trying to find my way out.

The cave also reminded me of something I wrote in a college notebook years ago while trying to keep a journal of my thoughts. Normally, the college notebooks, with countless lecture notes from my history or Spanish classes, were stowed away in a box and rarely looked at. Now, with time on my hands and a quest to find answers or find any meaning at all, I dug them up again.

If there is such a thing as heaven and hell, then it pulls at us— each one leading us down alternate paths. In the pulling, a third path is created and that is the path most traveled—some a little to the left, some a little to the right. The challenge then is to make something of the path and of oneself—to kindle and sustain a fire when left in the dark.

I thought back to the times I deviated from the path and went off course—skipping baseball practice, seeing other girls. Maybe self-sabotage is a desperate attempt for our true spirit to come out of our well-fortified shells—a painful, arduous endeavor using friction to connect to one's self; a way to file down your outer husk bit by bit; a way to access the real you, buried over time by the residue of life. You would think it would be easier, or that we would make it easier on ourselves. Then again, if it were that easy, maybe there would be no spark of life. "*We're all curious about what might hurt us,*" Lorca said, but we're not curious because we want to feel pain. We need it. We need friction. Affliction and torment, whether self-inflicted or not, remind us that we can only transform through suffering and sacrifice. That is the price of life. You can only hope that you are able to bear the suffering you create and that the weight of your shadow isn't more than you can carry. Otherwise, you might find yourself wandering in a dark cave and trying to find a way out.

Chapter 27

BPD

Not only can man's being not be understood without madness, it would not be man's being if it did not bear madness within itself as the limit of his freedom.

—Jacques Lacan, Psychiatrist

AT THE END of January, the police investigation had almost concluded and the shock had mostly worn off. What was left was reality, but the reality didn't make sense. People tell you that you're never really going to know why someone takes their own life, even though that is one of the things you want to know most. But with Rachel, there were too many factors involved that pointed to something out of place. After searching for answers on the Internet, both myself and Rachel's parents started to see her symptoms in the form of a pattern. That pattern took the form of a borderline personality disorder, also known as BPD.

One day I visited the NAMI (National Alliance on Mental Illness) website, and it stated:

[BPD is] a condition characterized by difficulties regulating emotion. This means that people who experience BPD feel emotions intensely and for extended periods of time, and it is harder for them to return to a stable baseline after an emotionally triggering event. This difficulty can lead to impulsivity, poor

*self-image, stormy relationships and intense emotional responses
to stressors. Struggling with self-regulation can also result in
dangerous behaviors such as self-harm (e.g. cutting). It's esti-
mated that 1.4% of the adult U.S. population experiences
BPD. Nearly 75% of people diagnosed with BPD are women.*

Besides the marriage therapist we saw that spring, Rachel also
saw her own therapist. Both therapists were like our trusted guides,
and we relied on each to help us navigate the rapids that carried
us that summer. Both therapists were good, qualified psychologists, and we enjoyed the sessions and appreciated the support.
Both therapists didn't know our full story however—only what we
shared in each session. Rachel told her own therapist that she didn't
have suicidal thoughts, which was clearly not the case. Both of us
never had time or the courage to get to the heart of the matter.

She told me once that both therapy sessions weren't enough.
She also told me that August she might need to be hospitalized.
Shame kept us from following through. It's difficult to admit defeat,
even when life has seemingly won and is kicking you while you're
down. There was also the issue of logistics and how she would take
time off. She had to perform at a music festival that weekend and
then there was the start of the school year. We tried to know the
right thing to do that summer. We just didn't.

Several months after realizing her probable condition and
about eight months after she died, I sat down to write a letter to
both our marriage counselor and her individual therapist. Roughly
ten percent of people with BPD die by suicide and it seemed like
she was part of that statistic.

On a rainy Saturday night in April of 2019, I finally found the
time to collect my thoughts. In front of me were blinds, normally
opened to let in daylight, but now closed and muffling the sound
of the wind and rain. The only light came from a ceiling lamp
above. I wrote the letters using a calligraphy pen I used to use for
composing music. Actually physically writing the letters allowed
me time to think and be more deliberate in my message. As tears

filled my eyes, I described what she suffered from and strived to help fill in the blanks so that they understood. Maybe they already knew. The one certain thing is that they didn't have all the information. The only person who knew more of the complete picture was me, and I was probably the wrong person to be in that position. I elected to be her guardian but felt like I failed. There was no response from either the marriage counselor or therapist and disappointment set in. Maybe it was wrong of me to write. Maybe they weren't legally allowed to respond. The more cynical side wondered if it was because I wasn't paying them.

Several months later, I actually gathered the courage to track down her old therapist from 2014 and gave her a call. My initial composed manner allowed me to explain everything as best as possible. I first asked if she remembered my wife and then said what happened a year earlier. More details ensued.

"Rachel made a lot of progress in dealing with her issues and she was very accomplished. But in the fourth year of our marriage, some of my own issues came up and it rocked her. She regressed to a more raw state from when she was younger," I said while pacing the kitchen floor and looking at the ground.

With a lump forming in my throat I continued, "But I just don't understand why she wasn't diagnosed with BPD or never…" At that point I broke down and cried while I continued to talk. It came as a surprise since I wasn't used to discussing the matter, and I needed a minute to regain my composure.

A short breath preceded my next question. "Was she diagnosed with BPD?" I asked point-blank.

"Words cannot express the immensity of the heartbreak you have been dealing with," the therapist replied. "And I'm so sorry for what you went through. Unfortunately, I cannot ethically or legally share any information with you. The only thing I can do is help you get the support you need to find some kind of peace and healing."

As I continued to talk with her, I ascertained that sometimes people in Rachel's situation don't want other family and loved ones to know about or be part of their therapy sessions. Maybe Rachel did realize she had the condition and tried to deal with it herself and with whomever her therapist was at the time. It was almost as if her own lack of transparency mirrored my inability to be transparent with her about things I wanted to keep private. With an absence of light, darkness takes over. The unknown face has the final say.

Amongst the many notes Rachel kept on her iPhone, she wrote down the name of a website about borderline personality disorder (BPD: Facing the Facts) as well as the name of the treatment commonly used called DBT (dialectical behavior therapy). She even wrote down the name of a famous NFL football player who suffered from the disorder (Brandon Marshall). In fact, she did bring up the player and his condition once in conversation years ago, but I don't think there was much talk about it and it didn't come up again. She also mentioned something about maybe having the disorder to her cousins around the same time, but I think it was again quickly dismissed. In the last year of our relationship, it seemed like Rachel felt most of her issues were relational and that if the marriage improved, so would she. The last book she read seemingly gave her hope because it helped explain our marriage issues in terms of attachment styles (*Avoidant: How to Love (or Leave) a Dismissive Partner* by Jeb Kinnison). She became excited after she read it and immediately wanted me to read it too. However, out of all the books and articles that she read to help her with life in the time I knew her, to my knowledge there was never anything about borderline personality disorder.

As I continued to research information about BPD, I discovered that it is difficult to diagnose because symptoms can be misleading and seem like something else. Also, there can be a tendency not to diagnose it or "label" the individual so that they won't feel the stigma or weight of that label. I imagine there are insurance implications as well. There were famous people who publicized their BPD diagnosis, like comedian Pete Davidson and the football player I mentioned before, Brandon Marshall. But my guess is that most people do not openly reveal it or even know they have it. That is why it is possible to draw a connection between BPD and other famous people whose lives ended early, though impossible to know for sure. People like Amy Winehouse, Marilyn Monroe, Vincent Van Gogh, Jim Morrison, and Princess Diana are frequently mentioned.

Unfortunately, while patients and therapists should include partners or family in treatment for the disorder, patients can opt out of including them, thus leaving people who could help them in the dark. This could have been the case with Rachel, assuming she was ever diagnosed. From the outside looking in however, it would seem she never really knew what she was dealing with. I certainly know I didn't, and neither did her family.

When someone with borderline personality disorder goes through a negative moment in their life, instead of being like a bump or bruise it feels like a third-degree burn. As I read information and watched videos about the disorder, things that once were fuzzy started to take focus. I now had an explanation for why Rachel would break down after what seemed to be a minor event. I also had an explanation for what she was trying to cope with underneath it all. In my reading, I came across the characteristics that qualify having the disorder. The traits of self-harm, suicidal thoughts, affective instability, feeling empty inside due to a void, and substance abuse were all present in Rachel's life, and those are the main characteristics of BPD.

To call somebody "borderline" makes it sound as if they're on the border between being sane or insane. Most are not. In Rachel's case, as in other cases of BPD, she maybe had the predisposition for the illness, and then her environment exacerbated her tendencies. Her fear of abandonment (another characteristic of BPD) was more pronounced than in other people, and my mention of creating space in the relationship and temporarily moving out was probably a trigger. Over time, she learned to manage her emotions and was smart enough to figure out how to present the best possible version of herself. But in moments of weakness, and when she could no longer hold everything in, she let go of that control and that is the moment when the borderline tendencies came to the surface in extreme reactions. You would have to be in a close relationship with her to really see it, and often it could be confused with drunken behavior.

I recalled the time she damaged my piano. She was probably beyond frustrated that I could be ambivalent about having children and her reaction was similar to road rage—a valid feeling, just not expressed the best way possible. I remembered the fight at the bar where she disappeared only to mysteriously turn up at home. From other psychology books I read, it seemed like in those moments of trying to publicly humiliate me she was reminding me of what she felt when she was a child and could not deal with shame from others—the same feelings and thoughts I tried to bury or run away from myself. She wanted me to know that she was the victim and that trauma she endured years ago was still there. Without a way to remember or express that trauma, she acted out.

There was of course the knife incident and the hitting. All of those dangerous eruptions were cries for help because violence against oneself or others is a repudiation of one's self—a belief that one's self does not matter or is inherently wrong. In my research, I learned that cutting and other forms of self-destructive behavior oddly do bring relief. They replace pain and intense emotions with a sense of calm and order. It's a type of regulating mechanism for when emotions are altogether too much, because a defining sensation replaces the storm within. In therapy, one learns to find healthy ways of coping that don't involve self-destruction or self-mutilation. In fact, one of the ways to cope with intense emotions is holding an ice cube and Rachel did the same thing once or twice while I stood nearby in our kitchen. I could surmise that she was introduced to aspects of the disorder at some point, but I didn't understand why she never continued learning more about it or why there was no official diagnosis.

People with BPD also were frequently described as using black-and-white thinking where no gray areas exist. This helped explain some of her overreactions and why it could be difficult to mediate conflict in the relationship. There was her comment in her note that there was no love in our seven years together and that my actions nullified our entire relationship. She was justified in feeling that I violated the trust and commitment in our relationship and that I did not truly love her. But how far did I go down that path? She later asked me if she was exaggerating things in her reaction. I told her that she was, but I also didn't want to make her feel like she was being crazy. Ultimately, it was hard to live in gray areas where things weren't completely clear. She wanted to know why I did what I did and wanted confirmation that it wouldn't happen again—all completely understandable. Even though I told her it wouldn't, the why behind everything took a year or two to answer myself, because I didn't know. She couldn't trust me because I came back from a divergent path without knowing why I wandered. For any couple, these issues would take time to work out and would be difficult. But when there's also a possible personality disorder involved, the ensuing path includes added peril.

Any person is so much more than a diagnosis and that is also true with Rachel. She was more human than anyone I ever knew. Questions swirled around my head often in the year after her death: Would a diagnosis have done her more harm than good—could she have coped with the stigma? Did she even have a borderline personality disorder? Or was shining a light on the dark part of her soul not even possible—was something else in charge of her fate?

Chapter 28
Grief

The borderline person's suffering has a telos, and this purpose, which is achieved by some but tragically eludes others, is also the telos of humankind.

— Nathan Schwartz-Salant, Psychologist

For the first few months after Rachel's death, I was in shock. There were so many details and questions spinning around my head that I didn't have time to process my emotions. But after the new year arrived and the free meals stopped coming, the pain and loneliness crept up on me more. I still attempted to think and process everything in a conscious way, which is definitely a part of the healing process. But the emotions sneak up on you. They often come out of nowhere or sit there lurking underneath until you decide you are ready to confront them.

Sometimes I got teary-eyed or cried in public. Usually though, my most vulnerable moments happened in the privacy of my own home. Something happened during our relationship where it was like I wasn't able to cry. I still felt sadness and despair at times, but couldn't quite express it like I could in previous years. It was almost like I got so good at burying my emotions that they were buried too deep to access, something Rachel knew better than me. That all changed after her death, however. I learned to cry again. In the privacy of my home when the feelings built up, I found new ways of crying I didn't know I was capable of. The hurt came up from within and the crying turned into a wail or a moan. There didn't seem like any other way to express the feeling and get it out. You have to though. The feelings don't go away and they need to be confronted before you learn to bury them or turn them into something else. I tried to find a home for that emotional pain, just like I learned in that Jungian workshop years ago.

Dealing with suicide felt like being in a hole. People recognize you're in a hole and often come by to look down on you and ask how you're doing. The irony or ridiculousness of the situation reminded me for some reason of a Monty Python comedy sketch from the movie *The Holy Grail*. Two knights are fighting and one knight (The Black Knight) keeps getting his limbs cut off. Instead of giving up, he keeps on fighting in a rather cheerful, British way.

"'Tis but a scratch," he says as his severed arm shoots out blood. Life was dealing him blow after blow, but for some reason he says that things are fine and continues as if nothing happened.

When people come up to you and ask how you're doing after you suffer a loss, you want to say:

"I'm in a hole, so things could be better."

But instead you say that you're OK. You try to continue as if nothing happened. The person who asks how you're doing often doesn't understand what it's like to be in that kind of hole. They're just glad it's not them. Some people are more empathetic of course, and those people often try to do things for you, and offer their services in some way.

The thing you want the most though, is for someone to throw you a rope so you can get out. You want someone to come by and help you out of the hole. You learn that if someone does throw you a rope, you still have to climb out of that hole yourself. You still have to find a way to climb up.

It takes a while to figure out how to get out of that hole. You're going to be spending some time in there, so what's often the most comforting is when people come by to talk and spend time with you. They may not know what it's like to be in a hole such as yours, but at least they offer their time and attention at a time when you probably need it the most.

The healing process isn't quick. There are some moments when the light shines through briefly and then things get cloudy again. At one point, I dreamed I was walking on a dock and pushing a large cart that contained a wall of stacked bowls of water, like fish bowls. I was sad about what the wall was blocking. There was bad weather on both sides of the wall. I next met a man that looked a little like the actor Jeff Bridges. He told me something about being positive and the next thing I knew, I looked to the right of the wall and I could see a great sunny ocean with good weather. I cried because I was so happy and relieved.

One day that spring, I was running on the treadmill in a nearby gym. I had gotten in the habit of wearing wireless earbuds while I was running, and I was listening to the album *New Life* by drummer Antonio Sanchez. The song I listened to was the title track, with its beautiful melody, vocal part, and a repeated piano line that carries the song. I had listened to the song many times before, but this particular time I remembered the Valentine's Day concert Rachel and I performed together with the Peoria Symphony. I imagined arranging the song "New Life" for orchestra and how it would sound. My imagination allowed me to hear the orchestra backing up the singer, and how powerful the melody would be on top of that. As I was running, I got emotional and wanted to cry— but not out of sadness. Relief and happiness suddenly overtook me. It felt like I was running in the clouds and a rush of energy shot through me and momentarily lifted the weight off my back. Each step got lighter and lighter, each breath easier and easier. It seemed like the ending of the tunnel appeared, and I wanted to embrace it before it went away.

The moments of light seem temporary. With suicide, loved ones and other people strongly connected to that person feel as if they're touched by death in a strange way. You go through life with one foot in the land of the living and one foot in the land of the dead. Suffering that is not transformed is transmitted, and so you take on some of the pain of your loved one. That is one reason why I chose to spend so much time trying to understand Rachel. I wanted to understand her because there were things she was dealing with that were now left at my doorstep. More poignantly, Rachel died that night in August, but there was also a part of me that died. It was as if we were fused together in that moment and I have been mourning the passing of our old selves ever since. I needed to know more about who we were in order to bring clarity and peace.

In the books about BPD, there were similarities between the people in the case studies and Rachel. Were they like me? No, but I understood what it was like to deal with overwhelming parts of yourself. As I continued to read, I felt a connection to Rachel. I wanted to read more books because the more I read, the more it seemed like I understood her and could understand better what she was trying to explain to me when she would tell me about her needs. The more I understood about the psychology behind everything, the closer I became to her. In terms of our relationship, we both had a common fear of intimacy and abandonment—we just expressed that fear in different ways. As I thought about her, I also understood myself better—why I was interested in her and how she represented something I was striving for myself. Even though I was never conscious of it, I secretly admired her for sharing so much of her inner self with the world. Sometimes I wonder what would have happened if I had shared more of my inner world, and maybe that was the point. Maybe she was such an over-share bear because I was such an under-share one.

Chapter 29
Reflection

Your joy is your sorrow unmasked.

—Kahlil Gibran, Poet

As I REFLECTED on Rachel's life, I could see that in a way, she was a modern version of Tolstoy's *Anna Karenina*—trapped in a society that seemingly blocked her happiness and trapped in a relationship where it seemed she had no control. Like Anna, Rachel used suicide as a form of retribution. The punishment was as much for herself as it was for me, because it seemed like her feelings captured her thoughts, and her thoughts ensnared her soul. Like other suicides, she offered a tragic form of mercy, since she seemed to think my life would be better off without her. Her lifelong, internal, philosophical question that we discussed throughout our relationship was:

What is the point of it all, if you can't have what you most want in life?

It was similar to my own internal question, just expressed differently. There was our conversation at the yogurt shop while dating years ago.

"That's just how it always seems to be—I get excited about something and then somehow jinx myself or I get overwhelmed," I had told her. My reaction to not achieving something or making progress in life was to disengage and become less emotional. Many times when my unknown face surfaced, I ran away and sought refuge. I learned over time to bury those feelings of disappointment and pour them out through my music. For Rachel however, and for someone who felt emotions so intensely, that was nearly impossible. It also didn't reflect the life she had led since birth—a protest against the cold, mechanical world we build around ourselves in order to survive.

During the year after it happened, I continued to write down notes in my phone. Anytime there was some thought or important detail, I wrote it down. There were always lots of small details about her popping into my head. One day I wrote down:

She used to say she felt like she was taking crazy pills.

She wasn't crazy. At least I never considered her that way. Her symptoms were like when people fight against a riptide. The undercurrent is like reality, and it can be deadly if you try to go against it. Those who consider themselves normal or sane end up recognizing the riptide, and let reality carry them where it may, until it is safe to go back to shore. But for others, they see the insanity of reality itself. They try to fight it, and it carries them further out to sea. After a while, some of them get tired of fighting and they sink. They see the rest of us living in an insane world and feel like they're taking crazy pills. That's exactly how it seemed when I jumped into the ocean off the cliff in Aruba back in 2015. If I think back on what that felt like, I can relate to succumbing to the forces within and without. They wear you down. At some point, you don't have enough fight left to defend yourself.

To really know Rachel was to know both joy and agony. Her normal self was joyful, funny, generous and loving. Her other side could be mean, resentful, unforgiving, and tormented—like the unknown, pernicious God we all must answer to. Life can be punitive, that I now know. We make deals with angels and devils we cannot see or hear. They wait for you to come around the corner and hand you the contract you didn't even know you signed.

In the months and years after she died, I had a hard time coming to terms with the essence of who she was. People are complex, and when they show you extreme sides of light and dark, it can be hard to hold the tensions of the opposite. The beautiful side was who she truly was. The other side was a side she created—a part of herself that was a reaction to the emotions and past trauma that overwhelmed her. To be fair, in a way, there were aspects of both sides of Rachel that she created. Her sense of humor was crafted to be the cool girl at the party. While she loved music and had an innate gift, her musical achievements were in part developed to receive love from her family. Both sides came from a fire and warmth—from an intense light she had within. One side was joy. One side was agony. Light and shadow is an eternal dance, and wherever you find the greatest light, you can also find a deep shadow.

In the spring, almost eight months after her death, I found myself in the office of a new therapist. He was the type that listened and added very little. As I sat on the couch in front of him, his eyes remained fixed on me like that of a big owl. Glasses covered his small, blue eyes, and what little hair that remained on his head had a thin, wavy texture. He once told me after a session that he appreciated my tenacity, but I was never quite sure what he meant. Maybe there was too much talk about Rachel, and not about myself. Since he usually didn't have conversation starters, I needed to dive in.

"In the early years of our relationship, Rachel would expect something from me or from life, and when that expectation was not met, she would be greatly upset. That's why I wrote this one song—'Reality versus Myth'. It's not to say that Rachel wasn't a realist, because she absolutely was. But she lived for what she expected from life, not what life actually presented her. Do you know that saying—if you want to make God laugh, tell him your plans?"

"Yes, I'm familiar with that phrase," the therapist replied.

"Well, Rachel used to say God was mocking her. Maybe like, someone was throwing her plans back in her face like a disgusted college professor."

"It is very difficult to get people with borderline personality disorder to see a different reality," he replied. "Have you ever heard of a concept called 'transitional space?'" he asked me. "There's a fellow named D.W. Winnicott, who I think had something to say about what you're talking about."

"Ah, no, I've never heard of him," I replied and paused for a moment. "At the end of our last session you said that God doesn't use people. But if that's true, then why do I feel like Rachel disappeared because I couldn't get my love life straight?" I asked him.

"Do you think that she had her love life straight?" he countered.

"Well, not exactly," I said. "But Rachel thought she had done everything the right way. She had been realistic and worked hard to achieve what she wanted. So why was everything being thrown back in her face?" I paused and looked out the small window to my right that acted as a portal to the outside world. "I could have said the same thing but chose not to admit it."

"Do you know that book by Jack London called *Martin Eden*? I asked him.

"Hmm, I don't think I've read that one."

"It used to be my favorite when I was in high school. The main character tries to turn himself into a person worthy of love and acceptance, and that was somehow similar to Rachel I think."

"How so?" he asked.

"She thought if she was funny enough, talented enough, smart enough, and pretty enough that she could win over the man of her dreams. It's just that it all got thrown back in her face, and she realized later that maybe she tried too hard. She was coming to terms with the fact that maybe she should have let things come to her a little more." I paused for a moment to collect my thoughts and again looked out the window. Meanwhile, the therapist's eyes remained fixed intently on me.

"I wanted to tell her to be patient—to understand there's a time for everything. That's what I did tell her as best I could. But sometimes I told her that what she felt wasn't correct—that her feelings weren't justified because they weren't based on reality."

"But feelings don't need justification. They exist because we are human," the therapist said. "What was her response?" he asked me.

"Just frustration. I tried to understand what she felt inside, but never really got it. Part of her inner struggle was what I reflected on when I wrote another song called 'Red's Song', since my nickname for her was sometimes *Red* or *Red Panda*."

There was a long pause and then after realizing I wouldn't proceed, the therapist chimed in.

"Perhaps it is the imperfections of our partner that cause us to love them," he said.

Talking to the therapist or friends was my only outlet that first year, and it provided relief. Rachel's struggle made her more human, and it was the same struggle within myself but something I chose to ignore. Even though those things about her could turn me off, somehow, they also drew me in. I didn't particularly like taking care of her after she drank too much at a party, but I got used to it. At least one of us didn't have to always be in control. She also liked to watch reality TV shows that I couldn't stand, but I got used to that too. She was my muse after all.

Besides therapy, I turned to books as a method of coping. One of the first books in my possession after Rachel's death was by New York Times columnist David Brooks and entitled *The Second Mountain—The Quest for a Moral Life*. My parents gave it to me as a gift and at first I didn't know what kind of message they were trying to send me. The first part of the book talked about people refocusing their life after a tragic event. The second part of the book talked about "Relationalism" and re-forming the social fabric of American society. Brooks argued that society needed to be more communal and less individualistic. He called for a society that turns outward, not inward, and made a case for repairing the mental health crisis through a re-examination of our lives and our goals. In addition, he reframed the concept of marriage and described it as a symbiotic relationship, wherein two individuals transcended their own selves in order to serve the marriage. Rather than an individualistic view of marriage, people should reconsider their selfish goals and recalibrate them for what's best for both parties.

Everything Brooks wrote about reminded me of Rachel. Rachel was all about expressing passion, sharing intimacy, and reaching outward. It was a part of her I was secretly attracted to and the part I was missing myself. I feel like she would have wanted to reform the social fabric of society by connecting with people and ultimately that's why she wanted to pursue a future career as a counselor or therapist. Rachel once said that she couldn't do as much good reaching people through music as she could through one-on-one chats, and perhaps she had a point. Rachel did not subscribe to an individualistic marriage and instead wanted a union where both partners grew together instead of growing separately, like flowers in different gardens. Unfortunately for Rachel and I, we were still at the point where the friction between us was supposed to create a new path. We were still in our separate gardens.

Brooks' concept of "Relationalism" meant that relationships matter and that they should be at the center of all that we do. Life is not a solitary journey. It is building a home together. This concept was at the core of Rachel's very being. Relationships sustained her, relationships motivated her, and relationships caused the joy inside her to pour out. Reading about her beliefs in the book reminded me of that part of her that would've been in both our lives if we had more time. It was a part I strove for myself yet remained outside my grasp—a part she tried to uncover in me. It is something I'm still trying to uncover, as best I can.

When I finished the book I gave it back to my parents and said they should read it also. Since they both were avid readers and watched Brooks all the time as a commentator on PBS News, I figured it would take them no time at all. Neither of them ever opened it and left me wondering why. Convincing people to do something has never been one of my strengths. When I spent time returning to my childhood home the year after her death, the staleness of the neighborhood reminded me that the vitality and sustenance I once received there were stuck in the past. The backyard of my parent's home was now more elaborately designed with shrubs, plants, and bark that didn't exist back in the day when we used to use it for playing wiffle ball or throwing the football around. The smell of desert sagebrush and the sounds of robins and song sparrows were the same, though those seemed to be the only things that gave me comfort. One afternoon, I took the dogs out in the yard and played a game of fetch with a rubber ball. They chased each other and tried to get the ball from one another, before Cookie got distracted by biting wads of turf and ripping them out with a triumphant shake of her jaw. My mom watched me from behind the sliding glass door with a silent, concerned look on her face. She stood there longer than normal, not moving, no expression. For a brief second we each had a view of the other, separated by a thin pane of glass, and the moment was an introduction to a reality beyond comprehension. Her eyes were always in the back of my mind. They were the only thing that had signs of life. The dogs and I must've seemed like we were in a different dimension, in a world she couldn't inhabit. Our realities were separated by a transparent wall, as if I was now radioactive and no longer able to physically occupy the same space. We finished playing and entered through the glass door which led to the kitchen. Both of my parents were by then milling around, aimlessly doing filler tasks like checking the mail or putting away dishes. An intense feeling of sadness welled up inside me. I wanted to give them a hug and tell them how bad I felt, to cry in their arms and break down the barriers erected over time, the barriers created with time. I almost did. Almost. I wished I had had the courage to crumble in front of them. I wished I had told them how sorry I was and how afraid I was for my future, but I was too scared and ashamed to accept something in front of me that had been there all along. We were still in two different worlds.

I said before that I wasn't able to cry around Rachel and that's not entirely true. On one occasion in 2017, I did break down and sob in her arms like a little boy—I tried to get out all the bad feelings that had been building up inside me, all the hurt that one endures when being brave in a world that doesn't quite fit you. It probably happened after she told me that one evening on the couch I wasn't capable of crying. When I broke down in her arms, she didn't know how to react. It wasn't part of our relationship dynamic and she clearly wasn't the most mothering type. In the end, when the moment passed, she made me feel a little foolish—like it was too much. That's probably why I couldn't express myself like that again with my parents in the time when I needed it the most. Usually you can only see part of somebody, and almost always, you never truly see somebody for who they really are.

Chapter 30
Going Forward

[Inner peace] cannot be learned by running away, by fleeing into the desert away from outward things; a man must learn to acquire an inward desert, wherever and with whomever he is.
—Meister Eckhart, Philosopher & Theologian

I CAME TO CHARLOTTESVILLE with a wife and a music career. I would leave without either. In June of 2019, after my teaching contract finished, I packed up my belongings and started a cross-country road trip that brought me back home to the Northwest. If I was only a Spanish teacher, then I might have stayed. The job at the school where I taught wasn't necessarily ideal, but the program was good and the colleagues were very supportive. I'm also a musician however, and there just was no place in C'ville for me musically. Perhaps I needed to be in a larger city. Or perhaps I needed to stop teaching Spanish.

The saving grace of the city was the people Rachel and I met. Charlottesville really did have a lot of talented, good-natured people, and it was nice to be around those folks when there was time to socialize. They were gracious, hospitable and very understanding. After Rachel's death, I didn't need to cook a meal for the next several months. People took turns and brought me food for quite some time. By the end of it all, I had a mountain of empty Tupperware and no idea who it all belonged to.

On my way cross-country I visited Rachel's gravesite that June, and it was hard to think of what to say to her. I had already said so much in those alone moments at home. This second return visit was less than a year later and included Cookie and Hershey.

"It's not that you weren't the love of my life. It's that I wasn't mature enough to love you," I said with my eyes filling with tears.

That statement came to me in the moment and it seemed to be a true statement for both of us. Neither of us knew enough about psychology or ourselves to cope with what we were going through. Both of us loved each other but had issues preventing all of that love to come forward. It was always there underneath, carrying us through difficult moments. Maybe we would have separated, but I think with time, we would have worked through our issues and with time, we would have made it to where we were supposed to go. Time wasn't what Rachel had however. Without hope for the future and with a dark unknown pulling her further away, she finally let go.

While I visited her grave again that June, I also visited her parents' home. Her bedroom was still the same and her mother had only gone through some of her daughter's belongings. At some point she brought out a bunch of papers from high school that were under-neath her bed. The papers lay on the living room floor in a heap and I helped her parents go through her past and throw away some of her adolescent thoughts. As we sifted through what was left of her life, a page from her fourth period high school psychology class caught my eye—a questionnaire by Colin Ross about dissociation stemming from abuse. In Rachel's answer for question #4 on the Dissociative Disorders Interview Schedule form, she answered yes to the question of whether she had ever been sexually abused as a child. She also answered yes to question #9 on whether another per-son inside you ever comes out and takes control of your body. This form seemed to provide some evidence for what went wrong but then again, we were all desperately trying to grab onto something that would explain away the inexplicable. When I found the paper, it felt like I found a clue to her past that I was never privy to, something she never really talked about. Her parents' reaction was silent disbelief, because perhaps they were also not privy to something that only Rachel carried with her.

In Rachel's death, she broke me open. For that, I will be eternally grateful. I am now somehow connected to something greater than myself—that something came from Rachel. I do not see life through my own eyes anymore, because I also see life through hers. I think back to the Tootsie Roll Pop philosophy that I first mentioned to her on one of our first dates, and I wonder why I had the shell to begin with. I know it protects me, but at what cost? Looking into the abyss that was her unknown face still makes me afraid, and I now know how hard she tried to protect herself from those demons. How then does one engage the genie in the bottle once it's let out? I'm still on a journey to discover how to do that— to confront and integrate that which is within myself. To build a ship that can navigate this night sea journey and sail where the waters entice.

Going forward after trauma or tragedy can often be more difficult than dealing with the actual experience. The person who listened and helped the most was my longtime friend from Seattle. I would also partly come to realize what Rachel meant to me by talking to him in one of our meetups. In a north Seattle bar called The Rock one sunny Saturday that fall, we each had a beer and talked about his conflicted, tumultuous marriage to a woman who also probably had a personality disorder, albeit a narcissistic one. His wife's name was the same as the girl I saw from Venezuela. He frequently called me for support.

The establishment had a U-shaped bar and that's where we sat at first, before deciding to sit at a table with chairs more comfortable than the toy-like bar stools. The booth where we sat was surrounded by brick designed to be in a state of disrepair. Even though the place was brand new, they tried to make it hip by giving it an industrial vibe—bricks at the top of the uneven walls were missing, knocked out, and almost crumbling.

"That's the thing. That's why I can't leave her," said my friend of over twenty years. "I always go back to my heart and it's leading me over a cliff." His youthful attitude was not indicative of the age now showing in his graying sideburns and baggy eyes. His short, athletic frame leaned into the table as he spoke with a beer in his hand.

After thinking for some moments I was cautious, careful, and concerned in my reply. "Your subconscious is what rules you, even more so than your conscious mind. You have to ask yourself at what point is it too much for you to handle—at what point does it become not worth it or detrimental to your health."

"I know what's best for myself and where I thrive," my friend replied. "Like, in my current marriage I'm not my best self—I'm not who I want to be." He hesitated, "But I always go back to her."

"But why do you go back if you're not who you want to be?" I asked.

"Shit if I know," he replied. "Probably because of what she gives me in return—she gives me that passionate love. Why were you with Rachel?"

"Oh, man. The same thing, what she gave me. I mean, we didn't have a super passionate relationship. But she was my greatest companion, friend, and advocate. I didn't think I could have that otherwise. I loved her for what she gave me and how she made me feel. It's just that it changed more towards the end," I answered.

Though there were times when our relationship almost ended for one reason or another, we kept going. I think it was because we knew we were both on the same team. The support and friendship we offered each other was too hard to give up. People form relationships because of a need and it's hard to realize in the moment what you're willing to sacrifice in order to meet that need.

We also talked on the phone many times. He called to check on me more than anyone else and continued to be the one person who constantly showed up in my life when I was going through

rough times. On one of our many phone conversations I confided my own personal struggles.

"How are you doing?" he asked me one evening. I always had so much to say and so much on my mind, that a conversation with me could take a long time—especially if he asked questions about Rachel. Whereas I could now talk for over an hour on the phone, that was almost unheard of before.

"I feel a lot of hurt and a lot of something I can't quite describe," I replied.

"You know how you said you felt like you were in a hole? Well, nobody is looking down on you. I think that's your own perception," he said.

"Yeah, but that's just how it feels. My life reminds me of the game Hokey Pokey from childhood. You know, 'You put your right foot in, you put your right foot out, you do the hokey pokey and you shake it all about.'"

"Dude, I know the game," he laughed. "I was a kid too."

"But when I put my foot in, it gets stomped on. What's the proper reaction for when that happens? Am I too sensitive? Is my foot really getting stomped on? Is there another game or a different version of the hokey pokey that I don't know about? Maybe the game is right, and I just don't like playing it. Maybe the game is to get your foot stomped on and keep going," I said.

"I think you're thinking too much," he replied. "Life is never going to be easy, especially if you overthink it. You just got to feel more."

"Yeah, but in a way, now I'm the one who is borderline." There was a pause after I said it as I tried to think about how to explain myself. "I mean, in a way, many people are 'borderline' in a general sense. The world now has less stability and meaningful relationships. That creates more 'borderline' traits."

"What, are you talking about hurting yourself?" he asked.

"No, I don't want to harm myself, and don't have any of the extreme tendencies of someone with BPD, but I'm dealing with at least some of the same emotions and anxieties. I cringe at trying to get what I want out of life because I feel like life is just going to pull the rug out from under me and mock me. That's how it always seems anyway—with my career, my relationships, my dreams. It's like I'm constantly at the shore trying to escape out to sea, but can't quite make it over the first big waves that come crashing down." I paused for a few seconds.

"But you know, now that I think about it—that's what Rachel and I had in common. It's one of the bonds that kept us together. It's one thing we always unconsciously knew about each other— that there was a part of ourselves missing and we weren't quite whole."

"But how do you know there was something missing? I thought both of you were professional adults," he countered. "Maybe you just had marriage problems, and she took it too hard."

During our conversation that day I knew that whatever was missing explained the self-sabotage and self-harm and that one's complete self does not self-destruct under pressure. That's what was missing. In both of us. There was a protective layer we couldn't quite break through, like a mask we had put on one too many times and couldn't take off. Something kept us from the other side.

When I go out for runs, I usually take the dogs with me. Cookie and Hershey have helped me a lot in coping with Rachel's death and I don't know where I'd be without them. Over the years after her death, our relationship has changed and we are now a tight-knit family, closer than we were before since I've used them so much for emotional support. Whereas before I was like their father, I later learned to also be their mother. At some point (I'm not sure exactly when) I started talking to them in the same voice Rachel used to use when she talked to our dogs. The voice sounds like one of those goofy, cartoon kind of voices, and it was something she got from the way her mom would talk to their family dogs. It seems strange that I would do that because I really can't think of other ways I do things that are like her. Perhaps cooking all of her old recipes because I'm too lazy to find new ones would be one thing, but I can't think of anything else.

I also recognize her spirit when I look at my older dog Hershey because sometimes he will wink at me with his left eye. I don't know if he actually is winking at me, but that's what it looks like when his left eye closes and opens really fast like a wink. More importantly, the wink reminds me of the way Rachel used to wink at me. There's something that's similar about it and I don't really know why other than it seems like the same kind of wink. Hershey also still continues to push his paw at me when he wants attention—a trick Rachel taught him when she was making fun of how I would give him more attention than her. She used to sit behind him, grab his front paw and push it towards me in a kind of mocking way, but in retrospect I realize it was probably a strange way of telling me she also wanted affection.

As the dogs and I continue with life, I imagine our journey will be similar to our runs together. Cookie will be leading in front, me in the middle, and Hershey will be following in the rear. That is how it's always been and I can only trust things will continue the same—one of them scouting the way ahead and one of them making sure we don't get too far ahead of ourselves. We won't always know what lies ahead but our path to discovery will be found by confronting what lies beneath—not by escaping it.

Chapter 31
Final Thoughts

I think of the night that it rained on the hill
I know my car wasn't safe sitting still
Swept all the trash cans away, the rising tide
Drive up against, or just stay, so I drive
Odd to see these things happening, yeah
They find you, find you
Me and my wheels could not grip, what was real
Right near the edge of the cliff, time was still
My universe made a split, didn't it?
It felt so nice to exist after it
Odd to see these things happening, yeah
They find you, find you

—Louis Cole, Musician

NOT LONG AFTER Rachel passed, I developed tightness in the muscles in my left forearm. Months later, my lower back had unexpected soreness and it was difficult to put on pants in the morning. I never fell over like I almost did in front of Rachel, but the process definitely took a lot longer. Almost a year later, I developed numbness in my right pinky—the same numbness Rachel complained about and the same issue she had a doctor's appointment for a week after her death. Instead of a typical doctor or chiropractor visit, I chose to visit a specialist in craniosacral therapy (CST).

To explain it simply, the idea with CST is that body alignment from the cranium to the base of the spine can get out of whack and consequently, unwanted tension and other health issues can develop. CST realigns the body and gets it to function as a whole unit while improving the flow of cerebrospinal fluid. I found it to be both relaxing and centering. The thing that intrigued me was that CST can also help deal with emotions or trauma and my particular therapist helped me unearth emotions I had buried somewhere in my body without realizing.

The therapist was an older man with a bushy mustache who was known as being a hippy guru of sorts. He possessed a knowledge of spirituality, as well as a conception of Indian religion and culture that made him seem like a retired college professor. What was more curious about the man with the mustache almost larger than his face, was that his main profession was making trumpets for the best trumpet players in the world. His last name was imprinted on all of his ornate, luxurious, gold instruments—but most people just called him Dave. For whatever reason, he also became a quasi-spiritual healer for any trumpeter coming to visit. A majority came with the pretense of wanting to try the amazing thirty-thousand dollar instruments. Almost all would eventually leave undergoing mental and physical fine tuning.

Since I had previously informed him about what I had been through, he knew other issues I was facing besides my pinky. The CST session not only realigned my body and eventually helped relieve pinky numbness, but I learned how to respond and listen to my body as a whole. It also gave me a path to facilitate the process of listening and responding to my emotions.

As I lay completely flat on my back, the therapist/trumpet maker tweaked my legs, feet and arms ever so slightly. The realignment allowed me to notice where I had been placing tension in my body—just beneath my right shoulder blade. He then got me to focus on my feet and do some breathing exercises that were designed to incorporate my whole body. As I continued to breathe deeply and feel throughout my entire body, a memory was triggered. I was suddenly back on the cruise ship with Rachel. One day, we had visited the spa on the ship to relax, and there was an incandescent room with a great view of the ocean as we sailed by. Inside the room were two blueish-green mosaic-tiled chairs that were heated. Rachel and I were seated in the chairs next to each other, holding hands, eyes closed, relaxing. Somehow, I was now back in that spot holding Rachel's hand, just to the right of me—similar to the time we held hands while walking in the park in Ketchikan. The sun cascaded in that day on the ship and illuminated her body at peace. I cried softly as I remembered the feeling of her hand and the feeling of tranquility that we had in that moment. Tears made the back of my head wet as they slid from my eyes like melted pain.

"I had a memory," I said out loud to the therapist.

"I know you did," he replied. "Rachel is right here with you. What do you want to say to her? What is she trying to say to you?"

His questions made me initially uncomfortable because I knew that physically she was not there. However, due to the memory I was experiencing I tried to reach down into my subconscious and answer those questions.

"It's so complicated," I replied as my right hand pretended to hold hers. "I want to tell her that I miss her and love her."

"What does she want from you?" he asked.

A minute of thinking and searching passed and an answer came to my mind. "She said she wants more from me," was my reply.

"That's good," he answered.

I didn't know at the time what "more" meant exactly, but there was definitely more healing, more searching, and more soul exploration that needed to be done. Rachel helped break through my shell, but it would still take some time before I considered myself an emotionally responsive person, or even my complete self.

About six months after the CST therapy, I ventured into a Barnes and Noble to find books on dealing with emotions in therapy. I inquired with a young employee, serendipitously also named Rachel, and she helped me find a book titled *The Body Awareness*

Book for Trauma by Julie Brown Yau. In the book were great meditation exercises that I used to start to tune into my feelings more—to
get outside my head and more into my body. I continue to use
those same exercises to this day.

During that summer of 2019, I was living by myself with the dogs
in a vacation home owned by my parents. I quit my job in Virginia,
moved to the home located in the Cascade Mountains of Roslyn,
Washington and tried to read and write as much as possible. Most
days after running with the dogs in the pure mountain air that
seemed to cleanse the soul, I would go upstairs, sit in a comfortable
leather chair and look out the window as I tried to recall the events
of the previous year. Luckily I had notes in my phone to remember
certain details. Each time I sat on the smooth, cool leather, I sailed
back in time, like a ship returning to the scene of a wreckage and
reporting on the damage. I tried to explain the inexplicable, to
capture a glimpse I was shown of an unidentified other, a nefari-
ous accomplice that was beyond my comprehension. Outside the
window I could see pine trees and the top of a house across the
walking path in back of the house. From my perch I often cried
in between moments of recall, trying desperately to confront the
emotions within.

On several occasions those same emotions tried to get the best
of me. Sometimes I would be driving my car on a mindless errand
and felt a strong bodily urge from deep within to crash my car into
the car coming at me in the opposite lane. The compulsion was
almost like a pain buried below that sought to either extinguish
itself or create more pain. It was something I only felt once before
when I was in the midst of the nervous breakdown/depression years
ago during graduate school. At that time, I was walking with my
family on a trip to downtown Seattle and felt the same compulsion
to hurl myself off of a nearby overpass.

Years later, now at the vacation home in Roslyn, that pulsating
feeling from within also visited me several times while sitting on a

couch late at night while watching TV. The malevolent compulsion from the depths of my soul would try to take over and I would be conscious of trying to live in two worlds at the same time—aware of the pain trying to push me towards something, but at the same time very conscious that doing something didn't make sense and wouldn't be beneficial. For the twenty minutes or so of being inhabited by this darkness I was forced to live in the tension of those polarizing feelings and forced to try to remain calm. I usually tried to continue watching TV but many times whatever seeped up from beneath was too much. I squirmed on the couch, stood up, moved my body, and tried to evade the pain that tried to either extinguish itself or create more hurt. Eventually, the feeling subsided—like the effects of a bad drug. I wondered if this was how Rachel felt in those dark moments that summer.

While writing in the leather chair I also listened to some of her music on her computer. It was the kind of music that I used to give her a hard time about because it wasn't my style. There were songs by Damien Rice, The Shins, Belle and Sebastian, Regina Spektor, Maria Taylor, Imogen Heap, and of course Gustav Mahler (her favorite classical composer). As I listened I could understand her vibe more. Unfortunately, it was a side of herself she never was comfortable sharing with me.

One song that stuck out in particular for its haunting rendition is "Silent Night" by Lisa Hannigan. It appeared at the end of a song called "Eskimo" on Rice's album titled *O*. There's a kind of despair that's articulated in the song and as I listened to it, I was transported back to that night of August 8th. The feeling of loneliness surrounded me like a dark cloud, and I imagined that it somehow reflected what Rachel was like that final night. Instead of the hopeful Christmas version of the same song, Hannigan sang an acapella version that's bleak and foreboding.

Silent night, broken night/ All is fallen when you take your flight/ I found some hate for you/ Just for show/ You found some love for me/ Thinking I'd go…

I silently cried, thinking about the last hour of her life.

The other song that affected me while writing came from Los Angeles-based jazz/pop musician Louis Cole. It wasn't one of Rachel's songs but something I discovered on my own. The song was entitled "They Find You" and it also has a haunting, yet beautiful melody. The song starts off with a slow lyrical string section playing a captivating chord sequence. It then transitions to an 80's-style pop ballad with Cole singing a mesmerizing melody in his signature high-pitched tone. While listening that summer and fall I felt the emptiness that comes with loss. My longing for the past and what could have been surged within me, along with the nostalgia ever-present with grief.

There was something in the lyrics however, that caused me to reflect on something deeper. What happens to a person when their conscious self can no longer cope with what comes from within? When what they feel inside and reality become blurred to the point of no longer knowing the right path. Rachel's emotions were valid. Her trauma was valid. But how did they shape her reality? How did they lead her down a point of no return? In today's world, people build intricate, sturdy exteriors in order to navigate and survive— like finely manicured yards that people spend hours preparing each weekend, or the technological equivalency of immaculate, shiny social media profiles that people craft in order to commodify their existence. They use words like "right?" every other sentence to confirm their assuredness and to declare that their reality is the correct one. They flex their super taut ego because it is the only thing they see in the mirror. The flimsy, fallible frame underneath however, always has the last say in the matter.

In Cole's song, his car is about to be swept away by the rising tide and he starts to lose his grip on reality. As I listened to the song, it captivated me and made me think how reality deals blow after blow until your conscious self is beaten into submission. In order to weather the storm that comes from within, one needs a sturdy ship and if you don't have that, you better hope you know people who can toss you some flotation devices.

People asked me why she didn't call someone in her family and ask for help—why didn't she think of everything she had going for her in life? The short answer is the normal Rachel would have done exactly that. In fact, she did reach out to a couple friends. But between 8 and 9 p.m. that night in August, something happened and she wasn't her normal self. Most likely, alcohol caused her to spiral and she succumbed to overpowering forces within. In my case, I obviously had family and friends who helped but I would say my flotation devices were my dogs Cookie and Hershey. That's who I held onto when I needed something to keep me afloat. To understand why Rachel couldn't hold onto them as well since they were also her dogs only goes to show the strength of what pulled her under. I thought back to the title of her poem portfolio and wondered why she didn't use the proverbial "bottom cushion for flotation." Maybe her soul was asked to join something greater than herself and her purpose lay beyond the realm of our understanding.

In February of 2020 I decided to move into a new duplex in the northwest part of Philadelphia of all places. Rachel lived there years ago when she studied at the music conservatory and it was a place she always (at least until the end) wanted to take me to visit. My journey by this point had taken me to a new city in search of a new life. I wanted a place where I could be myself and stretch my wings, so to speak, and I wasn't sure I could do that in the previous places I had lived. Philadelphia would hopefully entail playing more music that I liked, being better connected to friends, and finding a vocation that aligns with my true calling—essentially living my life with less of that outer shell and sharing what's within. Whereas before I felt like a toppled building constructed with shoddy materials, I now wanted to reconstruct myself—to create a stronger infrastructure and know the blueprints.

One night I awoke to voices. It was a cold night and probably around three o'clock in the morning. Frigid air drifted through the drafty windows and settled on top of my face. The voices that cold night sounded so audible that I first thought I was dreaming. Slowly however, I came to and realized the voices were coming from the neighbors' place on the other side of the wall behind my bed.

A man's voice spoke in a monotone, rapid manner. All that was recognizable was the rhythm and sound of the voice, not the words. He spoke sentence after sentence, all connected together, and finally stopped.

"I made a mistake. I messed up," a woman's voice responded in a pleading manner. She sounded desperate, as if she was trying to convince the man not to do something.

Again, he spoke his cadence of sentence after sentence with no change in emotion or inflection. He clearly had control in the situation and the control came from his incessant counter replies to the woman's pleas.

"No, wait. I'm sorry. I messed up," she said again as if something was about to happen. The voices quickly disappeared and they probably had gone to a different room.

As I lay in bed, my mind suddenly flashed back to the times Rachel would say similar things after one of her outbursts. I also couldn't help but think that somehow the woman's voice that night was Rachel's. The words would have been the words she told me the next morning, if she had lived. She probably would have woken up, realized how far she had gone, and immediately regretted her decision. Then, she would have felt guilty for the repercussions of her actions, and tried to do and say things to make herself feel better.

The truth is that on the first night in that duplex several weeks prior, the night I slept on an insufficient mattress on a cold, hard floor—I cried. I was so tired, worn out, and overwhelmed by my trip that I had an imaginary conversation with Rachel, who probably would have been disappointed with the place. In the months before she died, we spent many hours visiting houses and making offers on a new place to live. The place in Philadelphia was a huge step down from those Virginia houses and almost like living in a time warp with its antiquated British row house design and lack of renovations.

"I did the best I could," I said with tears streaming down my face. "I'm sorry that I couldn't find anything better." I later heard an odd scratching coming from the shared wall and quickly composed myself. I was alone in the room that night, just me and my two dogs, but maybe I wasn't—or maybe it was the neighbor's cat. So I quickly stopped acting like a crazy person and went to bed. I often imagined that the voice from the other side of the wall that later cold night in February was Rachel's reply. It was her reply to my sadness and to my situation. What else could she say? People mess up, people make mistakes.

While writing that summer and during the following year in 2020, I often returned to the thought of the small flowing stream from my childhood memory of Lake Tahoe. It soothed me, though there was something else in the presence of that water that gave me calm and peace. It acted like a wise, old friend, telling me that I didn't need to be afraid. I thought of my childhood and of other interesting things that happened previously in my life. I considered my own pain and the pain I thought I caused others. I reflected on my fear of losing people I cared about. Again, the sound of the water flowed around me like when I was younger. A feeling of tranquility washed over me at a time I needed it most.

The overwhelming sense of peace I felt also carried a message. Will future relationships and endeavors bring pain like they have in the past? Yes, but hopefully not that much—not if I can always return to this room with a stream running through it and return to this sense of having a compassionate guide. While pain and struggle can seem like it creates intimacy, it is only a reaction—a fear of something greater within, a desperate excruciating attempt to connect and create something new. Even though life forces us to move forward with joy as well as sorrow, hopefully greater self-knowledge and reflection brings less friction and strife.

On that day in August, Rachel broke me open and tore away part of my veils of illusion. Now I am putting myself back together again as best as I can. If grief acts like a stone cast into the water where the greater the emotional response, the larger the stone; then the ripples created from her death still reverberate strongly for me. They transcend time and space.

My own internal philosophical question was "why continue trying if your expectations or aspirations are never met?"—very similar to Rachel's own philosophical question. I built up a shield against disappointment and against being hurt, but that same shield blocked my true emotions from coming out. It also prevented me from taking the next step, a step towards being my true self and breaking through to the other side. My task now must be to confront my own pernicious God and create moments of light whenever possible.

Epilogue

He that dwelleth in the secret place of the most high shall abide under the shadow of the almighty.

—Psalm 91;1

THE COVER OF this book is a famous painting called "The Kiss". It was completed by the Austrian painter Gustav Klimt around 1907-1908—roughly one hundred years before Rachel died by suicide. It was also Rachel's favorite painting and she owned a large, six-foot tapestry of the image that she hung in the living space of all of her residences during the time I knew her. It was an understatement to say she liked the painting since she also owned a pillow with the same image, magnets that could be assembled to form the image, and also a decorative glass display of the image by Goebel. The reason I chose it for the cover of the book is not only because she cherished the image, but because it also depicts how she died.

In the painting, there is a man embracing a woman and about to kiss her. His head is turned towards her and the only thing visible is the back of his black, curly head with a green leafed wreath on top. His face is vacant, partially hidden, with only a glimpse of an eyebrow and a nose—what is on the other side is up to the viewer's imagination. The woman is on her knees, eyes closed, head tilted back, waiting for the kiss—her left arm wrapped around his neck while her right arm is folded over her chest. She is demure, he is expectant. Perhaps she is also imagining the man's face, or maybe becoming lost in the feeling of the moment; lost in creating the moment. They are both cloaked in an aura of gold. The man is also covered in a pattern of alternating black and white rectangles, while the woman is speckled with circular patterns of colorful flowers. They both appear to be standing on a patch of grass covered with a multitude of purple and yellow flowers.

If you can imagine a woman in the same position, but instead of on her knees, lying face up on a couch with her knees bent at the edge allowing her feet to touch the ground, then that is very much the last position of Rachel's life. They are the same position, the only difference being that one is supported by a couch. After finding her body that night, I placed her on the futon and called 911. As the operator helped me with CPR, I became the man from the painting—only this time instead of preparing a kiss, I was trying to resuscitate her. When the first police officer arrived, we moved her body from the couch to the carpet below and she would later die there alone while the paramedics gave up attempts at resuscitation. But when I look at Klimt's painting and I remember that night, I am struck by how much the two resemble her position on the futon—as if she still wanted to be held and embraced in her final moments and perhaps be brought back to life by a kiss—as if the painting that she saw and adored every day of her life suddenly leapt from her subconscious and became reality. I still own the tapestry and still place it on a wall in my new house. While looking at the painting one day and taking in its presence, it quickly became apparent to me that this was an example of art imitating life. It also seemed like an example of something beyond Rachel, something that became Rachel.

Nearly four years after her death, I finally retrieved the notebook where she wrote her suicide note. The police gave me a photocopy that January in 2019, and after years of persistent emails and enlisting a friend to pick it up and mail it to me (someone needed to be present in Charlottesville to retrieve it), I was finally able to physically hold and see what she used to complete her last act of desperation. At year four, Rachel's life was now mainly reduced to one box and one file folder of past belongings and sentimental keepsakes—strange to see how time erodes traces of a human life. For me, by year four, my shell was partially rebuilt again and my task each day would be to find any form of desire or spark that was seemingly extinguished from my heart. My emotions, previously raw and frayed, were now more cleverly buried and with each day became harder to access—the excavation and uplifting of my heart will take time. The retrieved notebook did not deserve to be in a storage locker somewhere only to be discarded over time, and it was the only item of hers left that still connected me to her. When I held it in my hands, I didn't feel what I would have a year or two ago. After extricating it from the land of the forgotten, relief came over me.

For some reason I always remembered the notebook to have a white cover. Now, as I held the pen that she used that had become sticky over time sitting in a sealed envelope in a warm, dark room—I was surprised by the gold cover that I could now see with my own eyes. The cover contained the same image from the Klimt painting, both on the front and the back. I vaguely remembered the book, and she got it in early 2016 since there were a couple innocuous entries from that time. Her only other entries were two years later, the day of her death and the day prior. By the time I held it in my hands, I had cried almost all my tears. I felt the cover with my hands and tried to remember her on that night in August—I traced the two characters from the image and felt the tiny ridge that protruded slightly from the flat cover. My fingers touched the book like it was any other book, only it wasn't. This Klimt notebook contained part of my life. It was Rachel's only outlet that night and no guardian angel came to intercede on her behalf. She deserved better.

Among the selfies Rachel took throughout the last several years of her life, there were normal photos taken at events and concerts. There were also more thoughtful, introspective selfies. They were the kind of photos that it seems like she took because she was searching for something in herself. There are selfies she took with each dog and in the photos it almost seems like she captures the spirit of the dog she's holding—as if in that moment she was able to somehow identify with the animal and create some kind of magical bond. Her face is positioned the right way, her smile and eyes look just perfect.

In a few selfies she took in April, her face is close to the camera and she looks different than the other selfies—a little serious, thoughtful, and peaceful. Her eyes are gazing right into the camera and when I look at the photos, I feel like she's looking at me or looking into my soul; as if the photos were meant for me or meant to reflect something about me. The only way I can describe the quality I'm talking about is as a kind of latching onto something; and I think she was so good at forming that connection, that her essence or her spirit still lives on. I can feel it in myself, and I can see it in others that were close to her.

When I was thirty-three years old, I was fed up with life. Life seemed to be happening to me and I couldn't quite master reality enough to affect any change. The heart is a lonely hunter and it was difficult to follow my heart's path when there were so many obstacles. That is a big reason why I moved to Spain. When Rachel was thirty-three years old (nine years later), she underwent a similar roadblock with life. Life was happening to her and she couldn't see past the obstacles that were set up. However, she couldn't leave. She didn't know where to go. The only thing that she knew best was how to latch on to someone and form a connection that would seemingly take her away from her dilemma. It reminds me of a poem that she wrote, where she borrowed some lyrics from a song called *Breathe Me* by Sia. The poem was entitled "Entrapment" and described her complex battle with an inner persecutor, or perhaps the way we all inherit aspects of our family we cannot escape. The line that always stood out to me is:

Be my friend
Hold me
Wrap me up

And fold me
I am small
And needy

Later in her adult years, Rachel was less needy than in her adolescence. But I think she still wanted to be embraced and wrapped up in another, just like her favorite painting by Gustav Klimt.

As we go throughout our lives, we think we have command over our destiny and our actions, and one could argue that that is true, except for the fact that there are still things that happen that we cannot explain. There are times when we are not in control and we are helpless to the forces around us or within us. I think a lot about that summer with all the rain, with all the trips we took and all the pain. The things she represented are still in conflict throughout the world and also within me. Mostly, I miss her. I miss Rachel dearly.

For whom does the bell toll then? It tolls for thee.

The End

⁓◦

Donations

WITH SOME OF the proceeds from this book and in going forward with my life, I would like to contribute to The National Education Alliance for Borderline Personality Disorder (NEABPD). This organization works with families and persons in recovery, raises public awareness, provides education to professionals, promotes research, and advocates with Congress to enhance the quality of life of those affected by this serious, but treatable mental illness. By supporting this organization I recognize that lack of education about BPD and mental health in general hindered our relationship and made it difficult to cope with our issues.

Links and Resources

NEABPD:
www.borderlinepersonalitydisorder.org

Donate to NEABPD:
www.borderlinepersonalitydisorder.org/how-to-help

Suicide and Crisis Lifeline
988lifeline.org

Mental Health Crisis Helpline (NAMI):
www.nami.org/help

Rachel Duncan Memorial Scholarship Fund:
myiwbc.org/rachel-duncan-memorial-scholarship-form

Gregory Duncan Author Website:
gregoryduncanauthor.com

Greg Duncan Music Website:
www.gregduncanmusic.com

If Our Hearts Could Only See (G. Duncan, piano):
bit.ly/3OMPjQT

Songs related to the book ("fashizzical" YouTube channel):
bit.ly/3ONA7mN

Acknowledgements

I WOULD LIKE TO thank my family for providing me the time and understanding to complete this book. I also need to thank all of the editors or people who read the initial copies: my friends Casey Nielsen and Brandon Walsh, as well as my parents and Rachel's mother and brother. To my main editor William Kenower I owe a lot of gratitude for pushing me in the direction of story writing, and to my long-time friend Rafael Guajardo, who edited the 4th version, I owe it to him for pushing further with the story. The PNWA (Pacific Northwest Writers Association) also deserves recognition for leading me to Mr. Kenower and for providing a window into the world of books, as well as helpful resources. Another great resource from my past who gave me good advice on the literary business was an old high school classmate and acclaimed YA novelist, Dan Gemeinhart. Finally, for helping me with the 12th version, much thanks goes to my other main editor, Anne Dubuisson.

To all of the friends who lent an ear and allowed me to express myself, I owe a lot of thanks, especially later readers of the more final versions. The organization known as The Dinner Party connected me to a couple support groups (one in Seattle and another in Philadelphia) that I utilized to deal with grief and form connections, so I owe them a thanks as well. Our marriage therapist and my therapists in Charlottesville and Philadelphia also lent an ear and did a good job of providing me perspective.

To Suncadia and Roslyn, the places I stayed while initially writing the book, thank you for teaching me to rely on myself for validation and not on others. Also thanks for the great scenery, free Wi-Fi, and free s'mores.

Lastly, I need to thank my Philadelphia neighborhoods of Roxborough and Clifton Heights for being my refuge as I sought a new home to complete this story.

Works Cited / Quotes

CHAPTER 2:

Unamuno, Miguel de. *Tragic Sense of Life*. New York: Dover, 1954.
  page 139.

CHAPTER 3:

Jung, Carl. *Aion: Researches into the Phenomenology of the Self*. Princeton,
  New Jersey: Princeton University Press, 1969. Pages 9-10.

CHAPTER 4:

Jung, Carl. *The Undiscovered Self: with Symbols and The Interpretation
  of Dreams*. Princeton, New Jersey: Princeton University Press, 1990.
  Page 28.

CHAPTER 5:

Rilke, Rainer Maria. "No One Lives His Life." *Rilke's Book of Hours:
  Love Poems to God*. New York: Riverhead Books, 2005. Page 49.

CHAPTER 6:

von Franz, Marie-Louise. *The Interpretation of Fairy Tales: Revised
  Edition*. Boulder, Colorado: Shambhala Publications, 1996.

CHAPTER 7:

Saint-Exupery, Antoine de. *The Little Prince*. Trans. Irene Testot-Ferry.
  Ware, England: Wordsworth Editions, 2018.

CHAPTER 8:

Robinson, James M. *The Coptic gnostic library : a complete edition of the
  Nag Hammadi codices*. Boston, Massachusetts: Brill, 2000.

CHAPTER 9:
Kalsched, Donald. *Trauma and the Soul: A psycho-spiritual approach to human development and its interruption.* New York: Routledge, 2013. Page 159.

CHAPTER 10:
Saint-Exupery, Antoine de. *The Little Prince:* Trans. Irene Testot-Ferry. Ware, England: Wordsworth Editions, 2018.

CHAPTER 11:
Neumann, Erich. *The Great Mother: An Analysis of the Archetype.* Princeton, New Jersey: Princeton University Press, 1974. Page 26.

CHAPTER 12:
Wilson, Timothy D. *Strangers to Ourselves: Discovering the Adaptive Unconscious.* Cambridge, Massachusetts: Belknap Press, 2002.

CHAPTER 13:
Neitzche, Freidrich. *Thus Spoke Zarathustra: a Book for All and None.* Cambridge, Massachusetts: Cambridge University Press, 2006.

CHAPTER 14:
Jung, Carl. *The Undiscovered Self: with Symbols and The Interpretation of Dreams.* Princeton, New Jersey: Princeton University Press, 1990. Page 135.

CHAPTER 15:
Opler, Morris Edward. *Myths and Tales of the Jicarilla Apache Indians, Volume 31.* Bloomington, Indiana: American Folk-lore Society, 1938

CHAPTER 16:
Hillman, James. *Re-Visioning Psychology.* New York: HarperCollins, 1992. Page 104.

CHAPTER 17:
Jacobi, Jolande. *Jung in Modern Perspective: The Master and his Legacy.* Ed. Renos K. Papadopoulos & Graham S. Saayman. Great Britain: Prism Press, 1991. Page 198.

CHAPTER 19:
Hillman, James. *Re-Visioning Psychology.* New York: HarperCollins, 1992. Page 116.

CHAPTER 20:

Hillman, James. *Suicide and the Soul.* Thompson, Connecticut: Spring Publications, 2020. Page 29.

CHAPTER 22:

Campbell, Joseph. *The Hero with a Thousand Faces.* New York: Pantheon Books, 1949. Page 391.

CHAPTER 23:

Harper, Billy. "If One Could Only See." Track 6. February 17th and 19th, 1997. *If Our Hearts Could Only See.* Japan: DIW Records, 1998.

CHAPTER 24:

Hillman, James. *Re-Visioning Psychology.* New York: HarperCollins, 1992. Page 33.

CHAPTER 25:

Estés, Clarissa Pinkola. *Women Who Run With the Wolves.* Trans. Maria Antonia Menini. Colombia: Zeta Bolsillo, 2016. Page 498.

CHAPTER 26:

Hillman, James. *Re-Visioning Psychology.* New York: HarperCollins, 1992. Page 106.

CHAPTER 27:

Lacan, Jacques. *Ecrits.* Trans. A. Sheridan. New York: Norton & Company, 1977. Page 215.

CHAPTER 28:

Schwartz-Salant, Nathan. *The Borderline Personality: Vision and Healing.* Wilmette, Illinois: Chiron Publications, 1989. Page 225.

CHAPTER 29:

Gibran, Khalil. "On Joy and Sorrow." *The Prophet.* New York: Knopf, 1923.

CHAPTER 30:

Eckhart, Meister. "The Talks of Instruction." *The Complete Mystical Works of Meister Eckhart.* Trans. Maurice O'C. Walshe. New York: The Crossroad Publishing Company, 2009.

CHAPTER 31:

Cole, Louis C. "They Find You." Track 6. *Live Sesh and Xtra Songs.* Los Angeles: Brainfeeder Records, 2019.